ENRICHING E SCIENTIFIC LEARNI

Jane Johnston and Adelaide Gray

One Week Loan

One Week Loan

Open University Press
McGraw-Hill Education
McGraw-Hill House
Shoppenhangers Road
Maidenhead
Berkshire
SL6 2QL
United Kingdom

email: enquiries@openup.co.uk
world wide web: www.openup.co.uk

and
Two Penn Plaza
New York, NY 10121-2289, USA

First Published 1999. Reprinted 2004

A catalogue record of this book is available from the British Library

ISBN 0 335 20393 0 (pbk)

Library of Congress Cataloging-in-Publication Data

Johnston, Jane. 1954–
    Enriching early scientific learning / Jane Johnston and Adelaide
Gray.
        p.   cm.
    Includes bibliographical references and index.
    ISBN 0-335-20393-0 (pbk)
    1. Science – Study and teaching.   2. Science – Study and teaching
(Early childhood).   3. Science – Study and teaching (Early childhood) –
Activity programs.   4. Learning, Psychology of.   5. Science
teachers – Training of.   I. Gray, Adelaide, 1973–   . II. Title.
    Q181.J58   1999
    372.3'5044--dc21   98–51884
                                                                              CIP

Typeset by Type Study, Scarborough, North Yorkshire
Printed in Great Britain by The Cromwell Press Ltd, Trowbridge, Wiltshire

Contents

Acknowledgements

This book is the result of a very productive and enjoyable partnership with each other and many other colleagues. We would like to acknowledge the particular help and support of the following people: Andy Mitchell of Bishop Grosseteste University College and Chris Johnston of St Mary's C of E Primary School for the the photography; children from St Mary's C of E Primary School, Sutton-in-Ashfield and Unity Primary and Nursery School, Nottingham for the photographs; staff and children from schools throughout the Midlands, who have evaluated the teaching and learning experiences for us; Nigel Snow, who has kept us sane throughout, with his patience and good humour.

Introduction

What is early years science?

Science is often described as a body of knowledge and associated skills connected to the world in which we live. This is a rather narrow view of science. Like all areas of development, science can be said to consist of three parts: the cognitive, conative and affective.

Cognitive development is concerned with knowledge and understanding: that is, scientific concepts and knowledge. They are identified in national criteria. For early years children these criteria in science can be found within Desirable Outcomes for Children's Learning (SCAA 1996) and the National Curriculum for Key Stage 1 (DfE 1995). Desirable Outcomes for Children's Learning is designed to provide 'goals for learning' (SCAA 1996: 1) for all pre-compulsory school age children. Children's knowledge and understanding of the world should develop as they 'explore and recognise features of living things, objects and events in the natural and made world and look closely at similarities, differences, patterns and change' (SCAA 1996: 4). For compulsory school age children, from 5 to 7 years of age, the cognitive criteria are embodied within attainment targets for Key Stage 1: Sc2 Life Processes and Living Things, Sc3 Materials and their Properties and Sc4 Physical Processes.

Conative development in science is concerned with the practical aspects or the development of scientific skills. Some skills may be generic ones: that is, they may be skills necessary in other aspects of learning. For example, skills of working together are identified in aspects of personal and social development in Desirable Outcomes for Children's Learning (SCAA, 1996). Other skills may be science specific and identified as part of the scientific process within Sc1 of the National Curriculum at Key Stage 1, Experimental and Investigative Science (DfE 1995) and Scientific Enquiry (QCA 1999).

Affective Development is concerned with emotional, social, cultural and moral development and is an important, although sometimes forgotten, aspect of learning. Its importance is recognized within both Desirable Outcomes (1996) and the Programme of Study for Key Stage 1 (DfE 1995), as children need to 'concentrate and persevere in their learning' and be 'eager to explore new learning' (SCAA 1996: 2), thus developing a sense of awe and wonder about the world around them.

Table 1 shows how scientific development in these three areas can be achieved through the experiences described in this book.

What is good early years teaching and learning?

Children develop their understanding about the world around them, including scientific phenomena, from experiences they have throughout their lives, and the evidence is (Pugh 1997) that early learning experiences are very effective for future development. Initially these experiences are informal, with children discovering the world in which they live and developing understandings and skills as a result. On entering more formal education, such as play groups, nurseries, pre-school groups and reception classes, children already have many scientific

Table 1   How the activities enrich early learning

Activity	Conative learning	Cognitive learning	Affective learning
I-spy ice balloons	Sc1 *Observation* Eng1 Language skills	Sc3 Materials Eng1 Vocabulary	Curiosity Working together
What's in the box?	Sc1 Observation *Sc1 Raising questions* Eng1 Language skills	English Vocabulary	Curiosity Enthusiasm
Mixing things	Sc1 Observation *Sc1 Prediction* Eng1 Language skills Ma Measuring skills	Sc3 Materials English Vocabulary	Curiosity
Recording weather	Sc1 Observation *Sc1 Recording and communicating* Eng1 Language skills Eng3 Writing skills Ma Measuring skills	Geography Weather English Vocabulary	Curiosity Enthusiasm
Why do things float or sink?	Sc1 Observation Sc1 Raising questions *Sc1 Interpretation* Eng1 Language skills	Sc4 Forces Sc3 Materials English Vocabulary	Respect for evidence
Body mapping	Sc1 Recording skills Eng3 Writing skills	*Sc2 Humans as organisms* English Vocabulary	Curiosity Respect for others
Sorting plants	Sc1 Observation Sc1 Classification Eng1 Language skills Ma Number skills	*Sc2 Green plants* Ma Shape and size Art Colour and pattern English Vocabulary	Curiosity Attention to detail
Observing around us	Sc1 Observation Eng1 Language skills	*Sc2 Living things in their environment* Geography Local surroundings Art Colour and pattern English Vocabulary	Curiosity Patience Respect for living things
You and me	Sc1 Observation Sc1 Classification Sc1 Recording and communicating Eng1 Language skills Ma Measuring skills	*Sc2 Humans as organisms* English Vocabulary	Curiosity Attention to details Respect for others
Baking changes	Sc1 Observation Sc1 Prediction Eng1 Language skills Eng3 Reading skills Ma Measuring skills	*Sc3 Materials and how they change* English Vocabulary	Curiosity
Dressing teddy	Sc1 Observation Sc1 Classification Eng1 Language skills	*Sc3 Materials and their properties* English Vocabulary	Curiosity Enthusiasm

Table 1 *contd.*

Funny fruit	Sc1 Observation
	Sc1 Recording and
	   communicating
	Eng1 Language skills
		Sc3 Materials and their
		   properties
		Art Colour and pattern
		English Vocabulary
			Curiosity
			Enthusiasm

Sticky glues	Sc1 Observation
	Sc1 Prediction
	Sc1 Recording and
	   communicating
	Eng1 Language skills
	Ma Measuring skills
		Sc1 Materials and their
		   properties
		English Vocabulary
			Curiosity
			Enthusiasm
			Perseverance

Flying high	Sc1 Prediction Sc1 Hypothesizing Sc1 Interpretation D&T1 Designing Eng1 Language skills	*Sc4 Forces* Ma Number Ma Time and measurement English Vocabulary	Curiosity Respect for evidence
Can you hear me?	Sc1 Observation Sc1 Exploration Sc1 Hypothesizing Eng1 Language skills	*Sc4 Sound* English Vocabulary	Curiosity Enthusiasm
Me and my shadow	Sc1 Observation Sc1 Prediction and hypothesizing Sc1 Interpretation Eng1 Language skills	*Sc4 Shadows and light* Art Shape English Vocabulary	Curiosity
How does it work?	Sc1 Classification Sc1 Interpretation Eng1 Language skills	*Sc4 Electricity and* *magnetism* English Vocabulary	Curiosity Enthusiasm

Bath time for Archimedes	Sc1 Observation
	Sc1 Interpretation
	
	Eng1 Language skills
		ScPoS The nature of science
		ScPoS Science in everyday
		   life
		History The lives of
		   famous people
		English Vocabulary
			The nature of science

Darwin has an Idea	Sc1 Observation
	Sc1 Classification
		ScPoS The nature of science
		ScPoS Science in everyday
		   life
		History The lives of
		   famous people
		English Vocabulary
			The nature of science

James Barry's Secret	Sc1 Recording and
	   communicating
		ScPoS The nature of science
		ScPoS Science in everyday
		   life
		Sc2 Health and hygiene
		History The lives of
		   famous people
		English Vocabulary
			The nature of science

ideas. These ideas are based on early experiences and may be only partially formed or scientifically inaccurate. In order to facilitate effective learning, future experiences should develop or challenge these initial ideas.

The process of teaching and learning in science, or in other areas, in the early or later years can be described as similar to baking a good fruit cake. When we are baking a cake we need to have the correct ingredients: good quality ingredients and in the correct quantities. We need to mix them in the correct order, sieving the flour, beating the eggs etc., and we need to bake the cake at the correct temperature for the correct length of time. Much of this process is subject to experience on the part of the cook: for example, in knowing when the consistency is correct for a good quality cake. Two cooks can bake different cakes using the same ingredients but both can be good quality cakes. When we evaluate a cake we do not count how many currants, sultanas or cherries are in the cake. We look at the final product. The history of cake making changes too, and fruit cakes of yesterday may look and taste very different from today's cakes, but equally good.

This is very similar to education, with the teacher as the cook, important features of good learning being the ingredients and the educated child being the final product. However, the analogy falls down, in that children are not passive in the process. Despite this we can state with some assurance that good learning is dependent on the interrelation of certain features. The emphasis on different features may change over the years or with different teachers or learners, but the end goal remains the same: in this case the development of scientific understanding, scientific skills and attitudes.

What features enrich early scientific learning?

There are a number of important features of the early scientific learning process. Each is important in enriching learning, but it is the interrelation of the different features that is important, rather than the individual features alone. There is no recipe for good early scientific learning. Each individual child, context or learning objective will affect the interrelationship between the features.

Learning is much more effective if the experiences are practical. In early scientific development, this means that children should be developing in each of the three areas of learning (cognitive, conative and affective) through practical experiences or exploration. Exploration is an important part of the scientific process. Through exploration young children may develop important scientific skills, such as observational and classificatory skills and the ability to raise questions (Johnston 1996). They will develop scientific conceptual understandings, which will be of greater use in their future lives than uncertain knowledge imparted in a didactic manner. They will also develop an interest in science and some important scientific attitudes, such as curiosity, perseverance and respect for evidence.

The more memorable an experience the more likely it is to affect development. Early scientific experiences should be fun learning experiences. The attitudes adults have about science are dependent on early experiences. Negative experiences fuel negative attitudes and negatively affect future learning. Positive experiences help to develop enthusiasm for scientific learning and this will positively affect future development. Experiences should be relevant to the child: that is, they should be 'real-life experiences' (Riley and Savage 1994: 139).

Relevance will aid development by making experiences meaningful and memorable.

One of the most important features of early learning is the interaction provided by an adult, whether it be a parent, friend, classroom assistant, play group leader, nursery nurse or teacher. Interacting adults have a number of possible roles in the early learning situation (Johnston 1996; Bennett *et al.* 1997). They may:

- provide the experiences, sometimes having a specific focus or learning objective in mind;
- act as an important role model by observing and expressing ideas themselves;
- interact with the children while they are exploring scientific phenomena, asking questions to challenge thinking or develop the experience further;
- encourage the children to express their ideas and look for other extended, similar or new experiences.

Through such interaction early learning becomes the partnership between educators, carers and child envisaged by policy makers (DfEE 1997; SCAA 1997). The importance of parents and carers in this partnership for effective early learning must be stressed. They provide valuable information about their children and previous experiences and can assist future development through communication with educators and interaction with their children in both formal and informal situations.

Using this book to enrich early scientific learning

The activities described within this book attempt to enrich early scientific learning through experiences for the child that:

- are practical, motivating and memorable;
- will develop cognitive, conative and affective learning in science and other areas;
- are linked to learning objectives for pre-school children (SCAA 1996) and children of five to seven years of age (DfE 1995, QCA 1999);
- are differentiated by task, outcome and support for children of different ages and abilities;
- provide guidance on the adult interaction to support and develop learning.

The activities are not designed to be exclusive of other scientific experiences; rather, they are designed to provide exemplars of good scientific teaching and learning and ideas for further development. They are also not designed to be used in a linear way as a science scheme might, but to provide some initial ideas and support for teachers to enrich the learning of children. There are many other creative learning experiences not included in this book. The cognitive, conative and affective development each activity can develop is shown in Table 1 and is not limited to scientific development. In particular, each activity will promote the development of language and literacy and may assist in the development of the National Literacy Strategy (DfEE 1998). The first five activities have a particular focus on the skills of science, although opportunities for skills development are detailed throughout. The next twelve activities are designed to focus specifically on the development of knowledge and understanding of the world (SCAA 1996), and show how this development occurs alongside conative or skills development. Four of these twelve activities are concerned with the development of understandings of the living world or Sc2

Life Processes and Living Things, another four with Sc3 Materials and their Properties and the final four with Sc4 Physical Processes (DfE 1995). The remaining three activities focus specifically on understanding the nature of science and the part science plays in everyday life.

Each activity is divided up into sections.

- *What before?* considers what experiences may be useful for the child prior to this activity. In most cases there is little prior experience needed, as these activities are designed as starting points. However, some prior experiences may be useful rather than necessary.
- *Resources* outlines the resources needed for the activity. Scientific equipment is avoided and resources are everyday and familiar, making the activities more relevant to young children and illustrating that science is all around us and everyday.
- *Language* provides indicative language development, moving from the everyday or descriptions using the child's own words to scientific language where appropriate. These words can link the activity to the National Literacy Strategy (DfEE 1998) by providing language for an alternative genre such as scientific communication or report writing. Scientific language can be significantly different from everyday language, and this can cause scientific misconceptions. Explaining scientific words and their meanings can help children to develop their scientific understandings. Science encourages accurate and detailed description of objects and phenomena. Having a wide vocabulary that allows children to make accurate descriptions will help them in observing and recording in science, but also in other curriculum areas. In the early years it is important to encourage all descriptions that help children to express what they see and understand about the activity.
- *How it fits* outlines the main foci for the activity in relation to national criteria for young children, such as Desirable Outcomes for Children's Learning (SCAA 1996) and the Programmes of Study for Key Stage 1 Science (DfE 1995). It also identifies how the activity fits into a topic or thematic, cross-curricular approach to learning.
- A brief activity outline follows the title of each activity and *Safety* or ethical issues are identified before each activity is described in more detail.
- *Setting the scene* provides useful information on how to prepare for each activity and *Developing children's learning* looks at how learning identified in 'How it fits' will be developed. Within science, this section considers how conative learning will be developed through a focus on specific scientific skills, how cognitive development will be developed through a focus on scientific concepts and knowledge and how affective development will be developed through a focus on scientific attitudes.
- *Supporting children's learning* details how the teacher can enrich early learning through teaching strategies and interaction that supports development.
- *Differentiation* indicates how the activity can match the needs and abilities of young children from pre-school to Year 2. Differentiation can be by task, outcome or support, thus making experiences relevant and meaningful for each child.
- *Background information* gives detailed information at an adult level, providing teachers with information on the scientific ideas underpinning the activity or information on how specific skills develop.
- *What next?* indicates further parallel and extended experiences which will develop learning, while *Other activities* indicates which other activities in the book will develop learning in specified areas.

- Further information for the teacher is provided by way of *Books/stories, Poems* or *Songs* that can be associated with the central theme of the activity.

References

Bennett, N., Wood, L. and Rogers, S. (1997) *Teaching through Play: Teachers' Thinking and Classroom Practice*. Buckingham: Open University Press.

DfE (1995) *The National Curriculum*. London: HMSO.

DfEE (1997) *Early Years Development Partnerships and Plans: Guidance 1998–99*. London: DfEE.

DfEE (1998) *The National Literacy Strategy*. London: DfEE.

Johnston, J. (1996) *Early Explorations in Science*. Buckingham: Open University Press.

Pugh, G. (1997) Early childhood education finds its voice: but is anyone listening. In C. Cullingford (ed.) *The Politics of Education*. Buckingham: Open University Press.

QCA (1999) *The Review of the National Curriculum in England. The Secretary of State's Proposals*. London: QCA/DfEE.

Riley, J. and Savage, J. (1994) Bulbs, buzzers and batteries – play and science. In J. Moyles (ed.) *The Excellence of Play*. Buckingham: Open University Press.

SCAA (1996) *Nursery Education: Desirable Outcomes for Children's Learning on Entering Compulsory Education*. London: DfEE.

SCAA (1997) *The National Framework for Baseline Assessment: Criteria and Procedures for the Accreditation of Baseline Assessment Schemes*. London: SCAA.

Useful book

SCAA (1997) *Looking at Children's Learning: Desirable Outcomes for Children's Learning on Entering Compulsory Education*. London: SCAA.

I-SPY ICE BALLOONS

What before?

Experiences of observing closely.
Experiences of describing objects.

I-spy ice balloons

Wrap an ice balloon in newspaper and let the children feel it and describe what they feel. They can also say what they think is in the package. Unwrap the balloon and put it on the tray. Let the children examine it closely, using as many of their senses as possible. Encourage them to look closely inside the balloon, to describe what it feels like and to listen to it as it melts. When the children have made as many observations as they can, encourage them to look at the differences between their balloon and others.

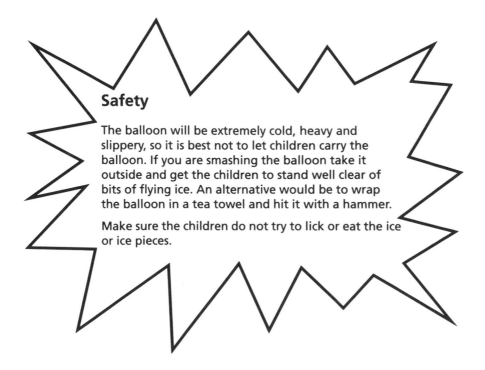

Safety

The balloon will be extremely cold, heavy and slippery, so it is best not to let children carry the balloon. If you are smashing the balloon take it outside and get the children to stand well clear of bits of flying ice. An alternative would be to wrap the balloon in a tea towel and hit it with a hammer.

Make sure the children do not try to lick or eat the ice or ice pieces.

Resources

Ice balloon.
Tea towel.
Newspaper.
Salt.
Tray.
Magnifier.
Food colouring.

Language

Hard.
Wet.
Frost.
Freeze.
Cold.
Ice.
Melt.
Float.

How it fits

With topics

Topics on seasons and senses

With National Curriculum

- Sc1, Developing *observational* skills.
- Sc3, Understanding how materials change.
- Eng1, Developing language skills.

With the Early Years Curriculum

Knowledge and understanding of the world.
Language and literacy.

I-SPY ICE BALLOONS

Setting the scene

Most children will be familiar with and fascinated by ice. However, they are unlikely to have seen such a large lump of ice before. Before beginning work with the children you must make the ice balloons. You could do this with the children's help but care is advised as unfrozen ice balloons can split and soak you. If you do involve children it will certainly enhance the ideas they bring with them to the activity, as they will have already made some observations about the unfrozen balloon.

To make an ice balloon

Take a rubber balloon and fill it with water from the tap. Take care when you do this as the balloon may come off and soak you.

Knot the end of the filled balloon and put it in an ice-cream tub (or similar). Put the tub and balloon into a freezer. The ice-cream tub will catch any water if the balloon splits while it is still liquid. The water balloon will need a whole day to freeze. The rubber of the balloon may split but this does not matter for this activity.

Developing children's learning

Language

Children should be encouraged to describe the ice balloons in their own words. Descriptions of their observations may help to develop understanding of materials and the ideas of melting and freezing: for example, they may describe the ice as crunchy (when it has been smashed) and slippery (as it melts). Other words, such as 'brittle', that help to describe properties of the ice balloon can be introduced as appropriate.

Scientific skills

The main focus for this activity is the development of observational skills. Observation involves noticing patterns and making links between ideas. Some of these links may be highly creative and so we should encourage these creative observations and descriptions in children. Children should be encouraged to observe the different parts of the ice balloon and to see how some parts seem clear, see through, transparent, and other parts appear to be solid, opaque, cloudy, murky.

Conceptual understanding

Observing ice balloons can develop understanding in a number of different conceptual areas. For example, observations of the properties of ice compared with water, how the ice balloon floats, the temperature of ice and how light passes through the ice balloon can all be made. You may wish to focus on specific learning objectives or you may wish to allow free exploration. Whatever your aims, the children's ideas about ice may change considerably through contact and exploration during this activity.

I-SPY ICE BALLOONS

Attitudes

This activity will develop motivational attitudes such as curiosity and enthusiasm. Children will also need to cooperate and listen to other children's ideas.

Supporting children's learning

Encourage the children to touch, look closely at and listen to the ice balloon, so that they realize that observation is not just visual. Some children may have difficulty articulating what they notice about the balloon, but they should be encouraged to describe their observations in their own words, and some more sophisticated language can be added. Encourage them to express themselves creatively, remembering that science does not mean that we cannot make creative observations. Visual observations can be enhanced through the use of a magnifier or by comparing two balloons. If a child is not able to see features within the balloon, such as bubbles or cracks, put a drop of food colour on the balloon to highlight them. The ice balloon will crack as it melts and children can hear this if they listen carefully. Cracking noises are especially obvious when the balloon is first removed from the freezer, but they can also be heard when salt is added to the balloon to speed up the melting process. Aural observations can be enhanced by taking a small group into a quiet spot, or using a stethoscope.

The ice balloon may have trapped air bubbles inside the ice. Encourage the children to say what the inside of the balloon looks like. You could ask the children how the bubbles got there. At room temperature the ice balloon will begin to melt. Ask the children where they think the water is coming from. You could also ask the children to say what they think would happen if they dropped the balloon on the ground outside. This will help them to think about the different properties of materials. The ice balloon can turn into a liquid but act just like a brittle solid. Try smashing an ice balloon on the playground (pick an inconspicuous corner and be careful of flying bits of ice).

The focus of observation could be a particular aspect of scientific understanding. For example:

Properties of ice

Here it would be possible to undertake a range of observations of ice and water balloons.

Discussion could focus on the similarities and differences between water and ice. This provides a good starting point for work on temperature and changes of state. The effects of salt on the ice can also be explored. Adding salt can lead to interesting patterns in the ice, which can be observed.

I-SPY ICE BALLOONS

Floating and sinking

If the ice balloon is placed in water it will float. This will come as a surprise to most children, who will expect it to sink as it is heavy and hard. Comparison with water- and air-filled balloons and other light and heavy or big and small objects can aid understanding of floating and sinking. Children can be encouraged to hypothesize as to why things float or sink, and they can explore whether something can half float or half sink.

Temperature

Children can be encouraged to feel the temperature of ice and water and make qualitative measurements describing what they feel (hot, cold, freezing, warm, temperature, icy). This can lead to more quantitative measurements of temperature using temperature probes, strips and thermometers.

Differentiation

By task: younger children would freely explore the ice balloon and make observations. The observations of older children can be focused by asking questions such as 'What do you notice . . .?', 'What happens to the ice balloon when . . .?'

By support: younger children will need more support from the teacher when exploring and observing than older children. This can be achieved by greater interaction, by observing with the children and by asking questions to support observations.

By outcome: younger children can communicate or draw their observations. Older children can compile two lists describing water and ice balloons.

Background information

The focus for this activity is the development of the skill of observation. Observation involves more than just looking. It should include use of all the senses, where appropriate, although obviously care needs to be taken. Identifying similarities, seeing differences, classification and sequencing can all occur as a part of observation. The skill of observation can be enhanced by:

- giving children opportunities to observe;
- encouraging children to use all their senses (where safe) in their observations;
- helping children to enhance their observations by giving them magnifiers, stethoscopes and other suitable artefacts;
- asking children to describe their observations, giving them new vocabulary as appropriate;
- encouraging children to look for patterns, sequences of events, similarities and differences in their observations;
- allowing children to describe the patterns, sequences and interpretations of events;
- asking children questions about their observations;
- allowing children time to draw details of their observations.

I-SPY ICE BALLOONS

Observations of the ice balloon may involve aspects of scientific understanding. For example, the water balloon has expanded as it freezes. This can be seen best if the water-filled balloon is placed in a tight fitting tub while it is freezing. The tub walls will prevent the balloon expanding sideways so the balloon will expand upwards out of the tub. The rubber balloon becomes very brittle and will often split. Sometimes the outside of the balloon becomes wet or frosty. This is because as the warm air in the room comes into contact with the cold balloon the water vapour in the air is condensed on the surface of the balloon and freezes into frost. This is similar to condensation on windows in cold weather. If the children notice this you could ask them where they think the water or frost comes from. Remember, they do not have to get the answer right.

The ice balloon will float differently from an air-filled or water-filled balloon. The water in the ice balloon expanded as it froze but the mass stayed the same. This means its density (mass per unit volume) will have reduced, making it less dense than water. As a consequence, the ice balloon floats.

What next?

- Look at the differences between an ice balloon, air balloon and water balloon.
- Observe carefully as you try different ways of melting an ice balloon. Try putting it into a bowl of water or on a tray, or sprinkle it with salt.
- Observe how different balloons (ice, water and air) float in a water tank or trough.
- If the weather is kind to you, comparisons with ice, water and snow can be made. This fits in well with work on *The Snowman*, by Raymond Briggs.

Other activities that will develop observational skills

What's in the box? (page 13)   Baking changes (page 50)
Mixing things (page 18)   Dressing teddy (page 54)
Recording weather (page 22)   Funny fruit (page 58)
Why do things float or sink? (page 27)   Sticky glues (page 64)
Sorting plants (page 36)   Can you hear me? (page 74)
Observing around us (page 40)   Me and my shadow (page 78)
You and me (page 45)

Books/stories

Ahlberg, J. and Ahlberg, A. (1978) *Each Peach Pear Plum*. London: Picture Lions.
Briggs, R. (1978) *The Snowman*. London: H. Hamilton.
Wilde, O. (1978) *The Selfish Giant*. London: Penguin.

WHAT'S IN THE BOX?

What before?

The development of a questioning atmosphere in the classroom.

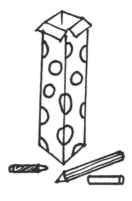

What's in the box?

Put a selection of boxes on a table, each one with an object or objects inside. Get a group of children to look at the boxes and predict what each one might feel like when it is picked up, and what may be inside it. *Do not* allow them to touch at this stage. When all the predictions are done, let each child pick up a box and rattle it, smell it, listen to it and feel its weight. *Do not* let them open it. Discuss their predictions with them. Were they right? What do they think is in the box now, and what leads them to that conclusion? Allow them to look inside the box. Was it what they had predicted? Does it explain what they felt, heard, smelt when the box was closed? You can now play a game to get the children to ask questions so they can guess what is in other boxes. Finally, children can use the contents of the boxes to explore a scientific phenomenon and to raise questions that can be answered through further exploration or simple investigation.

Resources

Different boxes (shape, size, colour, materials).
Different objects to put in the boxes (collection of pens, group of feathers, two magnets, a toy car, bubble bath, a brick, a stop watch).

Language

Descriptions using own words.

How it fits

With topics

Topics on Christmas

With National Curriculum

- Sc1, Developing the skill of *raising questions*.
- Sc1, Developing observational skills.
- Eng1, Developing language skills.

With the Early Years Curriculum

Knowledge and understanding of the world.
Language and literacy.
Creative development.

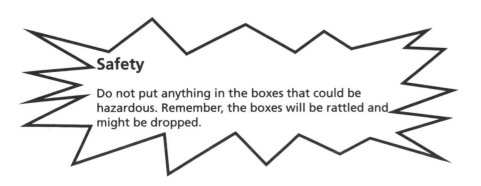

Safety

Do not put anything in the boxes that could be hazardous. Remember, the boxes will be rattled and might be dropped.

WHAT'S IN THE BOX?

Setting the scene

Opportunities for explorations and observations can lead to children raising questions, especially if they are motivated and encouraged. They need to be able to raise questions, particularly productive questions that can be investigated. This activity is a very teacher-led one and is designed to encourage children to articulate their questions in an atmosphere that encourages their ideas. Children can be sat on the carpet or around a table, and the teacher should guide them through the initial questioning and observation. The children can be allowed free exploration of the contents of the boxes before the contents and questions raised from the exploration are discussed.

Developing children's learning

Language

Children should be encouraged to talk about the boxes and say what they think they would feel like, using their own words. They may suggest the box will be heavy or light, rattle or sound empty. They may suggest what will be in the box on the basis of their observations.

Scientific skills

The main focus for this activity is to develop the skill of raising questions. Children should be encouraged to raise questions arising from their observations and experiences. Some of these questions could lead to further exploration and simple investigation. The activity also involves observational skills and making predictions based on observations. Encourage the children to ask if the box will be heavy or rattle. Once the box is opened they can suggest questions such as 'What will happen if . . . ?' or 'Why does . . . ?'

Conceptual understanding

This will depend on the contents of the boxes. If you put some magnets inside, then the focus for conceptual understanding will be magnetism. If you put some mirrors (concave, convex and plane) inside, then the focus for conceptual understanding will be light. With this activity, the focus can be changed according to desired conceptual learning outcomes.

Attitudes

The activity should encourage curiosity and develop enthusiasm. This will make it a memorable experience which should be long-lasting in the children's minds.

Supporting children's learning

There are a number of ways in which the teacher can support questioning in young children. First, it is important to have a classroom ethos that is conducive to raising questions. That is, the children should be able to ask

WHAT'S IN THE BOX?

questions without fear of ridicule or comment. The teacher is an important role model and if she or he has a questioning approach to learning, showing enthusiasm for new ideas and experiences, then children will be encouraged to do likewise. As teachers, we should attempt to improve our questioning skills and set an example for children to follow. The provision of motivating, new and different experiences or even different ways of viewing familiar phenomena can also help children to develop questioning skills.

Interactive questioning displays and opportunities to question and to listen to the ideas of others are important in creating the right kind of questioning atmosphere. Children can be encouraged to interact with the questions raised by others and to try to find some answers which they can share. This will enable children to see that there is often not just one answer to a question and that other people may have different ideas from them. It will also help them to develop respect for the ideas of others.

Children may guess what is in the box or how it will feel depending on the type of box used. A small box may not be expected to be heavy, or a large box light. A margarine tub might not be expected to rattle, while a heavy tin might. Careful control of contact with the boxes may initially encourage wild guesses, but as the children learn to use their senses carefully they will make more sensible suggestions and raise questions based on their observations. It is important to concentrate on one sense at a time and to raise questions as a model for the children. For example, if the box has a stop clock inside it the children may focus on their sense of sound and ask the question 'What noises is the box making?' If the box contains two heavy magnets stuck to the bottom the children may ask, 'Why is the box so heavy?'

Once the outside of the boxes has been exhausted, the children should be encouraged to explore the contents of the boxes and to raise questions that can be answered through further exploration and investigation. For example, with a box containing a stop clock, the children can undertake some timing, leading to questions such as 'How many times can we jump or skip in one minute?' If the box contains two magnets this may lead the children to questions such as 'What things will stick to the magnet?' or 'What happens if I put two magnets together?' A box containing some minibeasts, such as snails, could lead to questions such as 'How do snails move?' All these examples could also lead to simple observations or explorations to help answer the questions. The children can be encouraged to ask questions if the teacher acts as a role model asking questions and interacting with the children.

Differentiation

By support: all children will need support and guidance during this activity, particularly in the initial stages. Older children will need less support during the later part of the activity, where the children are exploring and raising questions from their explorations.

By outcome: the contents of the boxes will affect outcome and the types of questions raised. Younger children will be likely to make early guesses and ask more simple questions, such as 'Is it a car?', 'Is it red?' They may also ask non-productive questions which cannot easily be answered through exploration and investigation, such as 'Where does it come from?' Older children can write questions down, and these can be displayed on washing lines, interactive

WHAT'S IN THE BOX?

displays and question boards. This will help to develop a questioning environment and encourage children to interact with the questions of others.

Background information

Questioning is an important skill in science, as without the ability to question we would not challenge scientific thinking and develop conceptually. The age of the child appears to make a difference to questioning skills, with younger children often being more willing to ask questions, even though they may not be well thought out questions or productive questions. Questioning appears to be greatly affected by the learning atmosphere, the role modelling of adults and the attitude of peers.

Questioning boxes are an exciting way of encouraging young children to raise focused questions about their observations and predictions. It works by letting the children examine their own preconceived ideas, becoming aware of the way they think. For example, is a box that is small always light? Can a box still feel empty when it has something in it? What things let you know what was in a box? This is a form of meta-cognition vital for the development of hypothesizing and reasoning. It also encourages the development of observation skills and the cautious use of all the senses in science.

Children's questioning skills are not finely honed at an early stage. Children will have little idea of how to use questions to narrow down the possible choices, and they may guess straight away. This does not matter, but it will support their development if you encourage them to identify what clues have led them to make this guess and whether these clues could lead in another direction. Using the questioning boxes as part of a controlled systematic lesson will encourage a more logical approach through feeding the children information piece by piece.

What next?

- A flip chart can be used during initial explorations for writing questions. Children can write on the chart with large felt-tip pens and their questions can be discussed later. Decisions as to which questions are productive and can be answered and what to explore or investigate further can be made.
- Children's questions can be pegged to washing lines across the classroom to provide a more questioning atmosphere and focus attention on questions raised through observation and exploration. The shapes can represent the subject being explored, so that questions about feathers found in the boxes can be written on feather shapes.
- Question bubbles or speech bubbles can have questions raised by children written on them, and these can be displayed or brought to a discussion of the whole class.
- Interactive displays can pose simple questions, which the children can answer through observation or exploration.

WHAT'S IN THE BOX?

Other activities that will develop the skill of raising questions

Why do things float or sink? (page 27)

How does it work? (page 82)

Cross-curricular

Cross-curricular themes can be brought into the activity through the contents of the boxes, or the context of the activity. For example, a project on Victorians may use the question boxes to conceal a variety of Victorian artefacts, such as Victorian toys or household objects. This can be good fun, with the children being historians or archaeologists.

Games

Twenty questions

A child thinks of an object (animal, mineral or vegetable) and can answer only yes or no to questions about the object. The other children have twenty questions in which to guess what the object is.

Books/stories

Wildsmith, B. and Wildsmith, R. (1993) *What Did I Find?* Oxford: Oxford University Press.
Red Riding Hood.
Rumplestiltskin.

MIXING THINGS

What before?

Other predicting activities could be useful.

Mixing things

Label the solids and liquids with a number or coloured label, so you can recognize them. Do not tell the children what the materials are. Let each child choose one substance and ask them what they think will happen when it is mixed with water or another liquid. When it is mixed help them to see if their prediction is correct. Encourage the children to predict what will happen when other substances are mixed together. See if their prediction is correct.

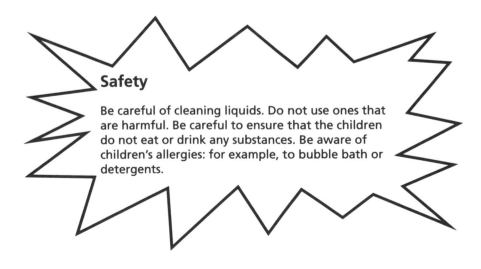

Safety

Be careful of cleaning liquids. Do not use ones that are harmful. Be careful to ensure that the children do not eat or drink any substances. Be aware of children's allergies: for example, to bubble bath or detergents.

Resources

Clear plastic beakers.
Plastic pipettes.
Liquids/solids. For example, you could use bicarbonate of soda, talcum powder, sugar, salt, plaster of Paris, cornflour, flour, vegetable oil, bubble bath (Matey Wizard is good), white vinegar, lemonade, water, lemon juice.

Language

Descriptions using own words: solid, liquid, gases, dissolve, float, mix.

How it fits

With topics

Topics on materials.

With National Curriculum

- Sc1, Developing observational skills, developing *prediction* skills.
- Sc3, Grouping and classifying of materials.
- Eng1, Developing language skills.
- Ma, Developing measuring skills.

With the Early Years Curriculum

Developing knowledge and understanding of the world.
Developing language and literacy.

MIXING THINGS

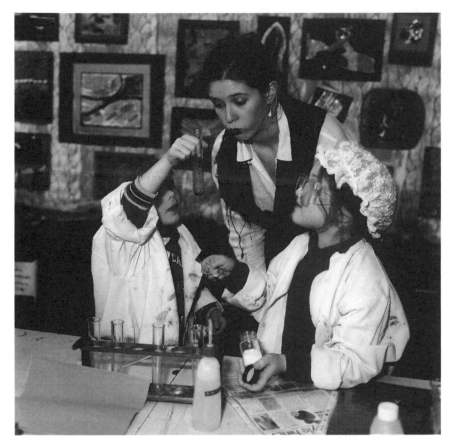

Setting the scene

There are two ways of beginning this activity, one being more teacher-led, with the teacher asking the children which substance to mix with water first and what they think will happen when it is mixed. The second way is more child-led, with children making decisions and mixing for themselves. Both ways need encouragement from the teacher to ensure the children predict before mixing and evaluate their predictions after mixing. It is important that the children do not see their incorrect predictions as wrong. They are also likely to become better at making predictions as the activity continues.

Developing children's learning

Language

Children should be encouraged to describe what they expect to happen using their own words. Scientific words such as dissolve, float, solid or gas can be added by the teacher where appropriate.

Mathematics

Children should be encouraged to use small quantities of the materials. This could be one teaspoonful or one pipette full of water. They could consider the necessity of using common or standard measures.

Conceptual understanding

This activity focuses on the properties of materials and how materials change when mixed together. Encourage the children to describe how the materials differ from each other, whether they are powders, crystals, solid, liquid, coloured, or what they smell like. They can also describe how the materials change when mixed together, whether they dissolve, mix, separate etc.

Scientific skills

The focus for this activity is the skill of prediction, which can be encouraged by asking the children to observe the materials and think what might happen to them when they are mixed together. As well as the skill of prediction, this activity could develop skills of observation, and interpretation can also be developed by encouraging children to observe the materials closely, describe their observations and the changes that occur when the materials are mixed, and attempt to explain what they have observed.

MIXING THINGS

Attitudes

This activity will encourage children to pay attention to detail and will also help to develop curiosity, which is an important attitude in learning. Unless we are curious about the world around us and consider why it does not always behave in a predictable manner, we are unlikely to develop our understanding in any great way.

Supporting children's learning

In order to predict, children need to have some experience of the world so they have some knowledge on which to base their predictions. To enable them to predict what will happen when the materials are mixed, they will need to observe the materials and consider what happens to similar materials in everyday life. It is often difficult to separate out the skills of science, but we can emphasize the skill we wish to develop. In this case, children can be encouraged to focus on what they think will happen by questioning and, with the teacher acting as a good role model, initially suggesting what they think might happen and why.

The children's first predictions may not be based on any prior knowledge and will possibly be simply guesses. As the activity progresses, the children will use evidence from the mixing of other materials as the basis for their predictions. It is not important, at any stage, if the predictions are incorrect. It is more important to create a sense of awe and wonder in the children so that they do not see the world as a predictable place. Some children will find it difficult to make predictions. The teacher can support these children and make some suggestions for the children to choose from.

Children are likely to use large quantities of materials when mixing, and it is sensible for the teacher to encourage them to use small amounts of the materials to mix together and to use the same amount of each material, although this is not essential. It is not important for the children to know what the materials are, as this helps to create the interest. However, you could inform them after the activity is completed and encourage them to find other materials to test.

Differentiation

By support: for younger children the activity will be better if it is teacher-supported and very exploratory. For older children the activity can be more child-led and investigative, with a methodical approach.

By outcome: for younger children recording should be oral, discussing their results with others. Older children could produce a table that records their predictions and identifies what happens to different materials when mixed.

Background information

The skill of prediction is based on observation, and children will bring their own experiences and knowledge to this activity, thus altering the accuracy of their predictions. The skill of prediction leads to testing and hypothesizing, and as such is an important prerequisite to future experimentation and investigation.

There will be different reactions when different solids and liquids are mixed. Matey Wizard bubble bath changes colour with materials of different acidity. Acid materials include vinegar and lemon juice. Alkaline materials include bicarbonate of soda and detergent. Bicarbonate of soda will fizz when mixed with vinegar as there is a chemical reaction which releases carbon dioxide. Oil and water will not mix as the water is denser than the oil. Sugar and salt dissolve in water and mixing water with plaster of Paris involves a chemical reaction as it solidifies, and there is a heat transfer. Cornflour forms a liquid unless under stress (that is, when you press it or hit it or pick it up and squeeze it), when it appears to break or crack. This is due to the small particles in the cornflour. Flour and talcum powder clump when mixed with water.

What next?

- Allow the children to pretend to be chemists and mix different substances to make a new medicine.
- Bake a cake and predict the changes that will occur when mixing or heating.
- Try estimating measures. This can take place in the water trough or sand tray or when baking.

Other activities that will develop prediction skills

Baking changes (page 50)   What's in the box? (page 13)
Sticky glues (page 64)   Flying high (page 69)
Recording weather (page 22)

Books/stories

Dahl, R. (1981) *George's Marvellous Medicine*. Harmondsworth: Puffin.

RECORDING WEATHER

What before?

Observations of the weather and seasonal changes.

Resources

Pens.
Paper.
Squared paper.
A clear beaker.
A flag or scarf.
A tape recorder and tape.
A large thermometer, temperature strip or probe.

Recording weather

Allow the children to make observations of the weather over a period of time. You can use various techniques to help you observe the weather. For example, you could use a beaker to measure the rain, or chalk or paint the outline of puddles to see how the weather has caused the puddles to shrink or grow. A flag can be used to measure the wind or a tape recorder to record the wind in trees, and a thermometer to measure the temperature. Observe the clouds. Ask the children to describe the weather in their own words, introducing new ones where appropriate. Discuss symbols that can represent the different weather conditions and use these to represent the weather on a daily chart.

Language

Descriptions of the weather using own words: cloud, fog, wind, rain, sleet, hail, snow, sunny, hot, cold.

For older children measuring words can be introduced, such as millilitres and degrees Celsius.

How it fits

With topics

Topics on the environment, weather and seasons.

With National Curriculum

- Sc1, Developing the skills of *recording and communicating*.
- Sc1, Developing observational skills.
- Geog, Developing understanding of the weather in the immediate locality.
- Eng1, Developing language skills.

For older children

- Eng3, Developing writing skills.
- Ma, Developing measuring skills.

With the Early Years Curriculum

Knowledge and understanding of the world.
Language and literacy.

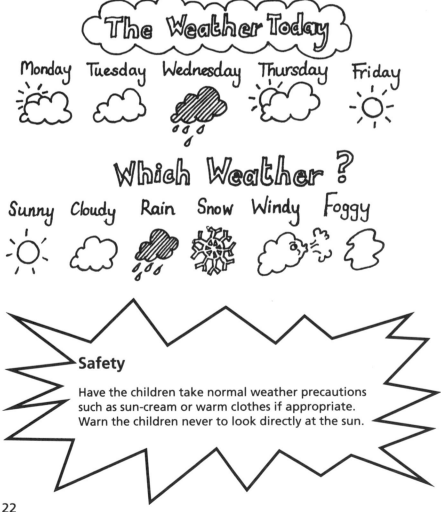

The Weather Today

Monday | Tuesday | Wednesday | Thursday | Friday

Which Weather?

Sunny | Cloudy | Rain | Snow | Windy | Foggy

Safety

Have the children take normal weather precautions such as sun-cream or warm clothes if appropriate. Warn the children never to look directly at the sun.

RECORDING WEATHER

Setting the scene

The focus for this activity is on recording and communicating the observations made about the weather. Obviously, the children need actually to observe the weather to do this, and could even take measurements of the weather. The recording of the weather for each day could be child- or teacher-need actually to observe the weather to do this, and could even take measurements of the weather. The recording of the weather for each day could be child- or teacher-led and a whole-class activity. Recording could take place at the start, middle or end of each school day. Alternatively, a small group could do a weather report each day to share with the others in the class.

Developing children's learning

Language

Encourage the children to describe the weather using their own words. Remember, these words can be very creative and not necessarily scientific. Where appropriate, introduce weather words such as wind, fog, snow, hail and so on.

Mathematics

Older children can be encouraged to measure the weather either qualitatively or more quantitatively. For example, children can feel how hot it is compared to yesterday or they can use simple thermometers or temperature sensors. They can collect the rain in beakers and measure the water using standard or non-standard measures. They can feel the wind on their skin, tape the noise the wind makes in the leaves of a tree or see how it blows a flag or scarf.

Scientific skills

Children should be encouraged to record their observations of the weather in simple drawings on charts and tables. They could use symbols to describe the weather conditions and/or write their observations on a chart. The chart could be individual or a class one, and could be permanent or reusable (using stick-on symbols). The children should be encouraged to communicate their observations and weather records to others.

Conceptual understanding

Understanding of weather conditions is mainly a geographical concept, although in science it is necessary to understand seasonal changes in the weather and their effects on plants and animals (Sc2) and how materials weather (Sc3).

Attitudes

This activity would help to develop curiosity and enthusiasm, especially if the children were involved in role play as weathermen.

RECORDING WEATHER

Supporting children's learning

Encourage the children to articulate what they observe in the weather. Help them to see the differences in the weather conditions throughout a day and from day to day. Introduce words to describe the weather and make sure that they have a common understanding of the words.

Discussing the weather is a suitable recording and communicating method for some children, but recording skills can be developed further by:

- Allowing children time to discuss weather conditions with each other.
- Encouraging children to use symbols to record different weather conditions.
- Encouraging older children to write descriptions of the weather, and measure rainfall and temperature.
- Use data collected from observations and measurements to make pictograms, simple bar charts and tables.
- Displaying records of weather so that patterns in the weather conditions can be seen and interpretations can be made.
- Allowing children to present their findings to others. This could be orally, by showing charts and tables or by being weather men and making a video or tape recording of their weather summary or forecast for the day.

Differentiation

By task: with younger children you could focus on one aspect of the weather and think of as many ways to record this as possible. Monitoring of the weather should be qualitative in nature, and recording and communicating should be oral, pictorial and simple. The simplest record would be a large daily chart, with weather symbols that could be stuck on, or a laminated chart on which the children could draw symbols using overhead transparency pens. This could develop into a weekly pictogram of the weather.

Older children could become more quantitative in their monitoring of weather conditions and then can record all aspects of the weather using charts, tables, bar graphs etc. These could be in drawn or written format, and displayed or presented orally to others in class presentations or weather forecasting videos or tape recordings.

Background information

Recording and communicating are important parts of the scientific process. Children need to be able to record data from an exploration or investigation in order to interpret from them and understand a concept more thoroughly. Recording and communicating can take a variety of different forms, some being more formal than others. We often focus on recording and communicating in a written or drawn format. There are some dangers when this happens. One is that the recording and communicating of a science activity can dominate in terms of time allocation but have little effect on understanding. For recording and communicating to be effective it needs to be purposeful, assisting in the achievement of the learning objective. Recording also needs to be varied, so that it does not become a meaningless and uninteresting end to an activity. Another danger is that recording and communicating in a written format can be seen as a necessary means of assessing understanding, as well as evidence that an area of learning has been covered. We need to remember that the recorded work can give us an indication of the child's understanding, but a full picture can only be obtained using a variety of assessment techniques, such as observation, questioning and discussion. If we focus on written or drawn recording of work, then children can often see science only as the end product, and the awe and wonder of science and motivation for learning is diminished.

There are a number of very valuable recording methods that we can use with young children, and we should attempt to use a variety of different methods. All are designed to develop the skill of recording as well as develop understanding of weather conditions:

- discussion of weather conditions in small or large groups;
- using symbols to represent weather conditions;
- keeping a record of weather conditions over time, using symbols or writing;
- keeping a record of measurements made in charts, tables or pictograms;
- communicating weather reports to others orally or through displays, video or tape recordings;
- recording could also involve pictures of the weather cut out from newspapers or the clothes you associate with a certain type of weather.

The Internet has several sites that allow you direct access to satellite pictures, which record the weather over the past few hours. This can give you up-to-date weather information, and it could be interesting for children to see the weather they have experienced from space, and to relate it to weather in other countries or other parts of Britain.

What next?

- Use simple sensors to measure the weather changes over time. Some data-logging packages are suitable for use with early years children and show weather changes over time.
- Record the weather over a longer time, especially in autumn or spring, when the weather is very changeable.
- Observe different cloud types, and encourage the children to say what they look like and draw them.
- Listen to the shipping forecast.
- Try out different techniques, perhaps suggested by the children, for monitoring and measuring the weather. This could be a new Beaufort scale or a new rain scale.
- Role play as weather forecasters by creating a weather station in the classroom.
- Use the Internet to find weather sites and weather maps.

Other activities that would develop the skill of recording and communicating

Body mapping (page 31)
Sorting plants (page 36)
You and me (page 45)

Funny fruit (page 58)
Sticky glues (page 64)

RECORDING WEATHER

Other activities that would develop knowledge and understanding of the weather and seasonal changes

Dressing teddy (page 54)   Me and my shadow (page 78)
Observing around us (page 40)

Books/stories

Pieňkowski, J. (1979) *Weather*. London: Heinemann.

Sayings

'Red sky at night, shepherd's delight, Red sky in the morning, shepherd's warning.' What do these sayings mean? Can you think of some more?

Songs

Drip Drip Drop Little April Showers.
The Sun Has Got His Hat on.

Poems

Whether the weather be fine,
Or whether the weather be not,
Whether the weather be cold,
Or whether the weather be hot,
We'll weather the weather,
Whatever the weather,
Whether we like it or not.

***

Rain, by Robert Louis Stevenson

The rain is raining all around,
It falls on field and tree,

It rains on the umbrellas here,
And on the ships at sea.

Internet information

www.nottingham.ac.uk/meteostat/
www.meto.govt.uk/

WHY DO THINGS FLOAT OR SINK?

What before?

Experience of water play.

Floating and sinking

Allow the children to explore the objects in the water trough. You can ask them to predict what will happen to the objects when they put them into the water before their exploration. Ask them questions to focus on their observation of what happens to the objects in the water, and encourage them to give explanations of why some objects float and some sink.

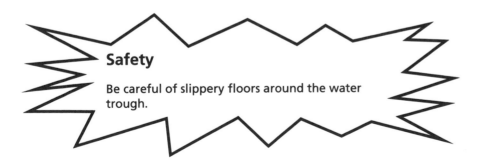

Safety

Be careful of slippery floors around the water trough.

Resources

Water trough or plastic tank.
A set of objects which float or sink. You could include: a cork, a pair of scissors, some Plasticine, a pine cone, a plastic bottle, some aluminium foil, a plastic beaker, an orange, an ice balloon, a water-filled balloon, an air-filled balloon.

Language

Float.
Sink.
Big.
Small.
(Heavy, light can also be introduced in conjunction with big and small.)

How it fits

With topics

Topics on water and boats.

With National Curriculum

- Sc1, Developing observational skills.
- Sc1, Developing the skill of raising questions.
- Sc1, Developing *interpretation* skills.
- Sc4, Developing understanding the forces involved in floating and sinking.
- Sc3, Developing understanding of materials and their properties.
- Eng1, Developing language skills.

With the Early Years Curriculum

Knowledge and understanding of the world.
Language and literacy.

WHY DO THINGS FLOAT OR SINK?

Setting the scene

This activity can be an extension to normal water play. Begin the activity by allowing the children free exploration of the objects and then focus their attention on observations. The focus of the activity is interpretation, so it is essential to allow time to discuss the children's ideas during and after the activity. Carpet time can be used to discuss different interpretations of observations.

Developing children's learning

Language

Children should be encouraged to describe their observations and interpretations of floating and sinking using their own words. More specific words, such as big, small, heavy for size and light for size, can be introduced by the teacher during the activity.

Scientific skills

The main focus for this activity is to develop the skill of interpretation. Children should be encouraged to observe floating and sinking in action and provide some interpretation for what they observe. The children will develop some simple hypotheses based on their observations, but these will not always be correct. It is not important for children to come to the correct scientific interpretation of events at this age, but more important that they are using their observations of scientific phenomena to come to some reasonable interpretations of how the world works.

Conceptual understanding

There are two scientific concepts which affect floating and sinking: forces and materials and their properties. Observation and exploration of floating and sinking can help to develop understanding of the forces involved in floating and sinking and the effect of different materials on the way they float or sink.

Attitudes

It is important that children's incorrect ideas are challenged through exploration and observation. When faced with such experiences, children are often unwilling to accept the evidence. This activity will help children to develop respect for evidence and to reconsider their ideas.

WHY DO THINGS FLOAT OR SINK?

Supporting children's learning

Allow the children some free time to explore the resources and then encourage them in their exploration by being a good role model and by your own enthusiasm. Ask questions to encourage their exploration, observation and question raising, such as 'Does this float or sink?', 'What could you find out about . . . ?', 'How could you make this float/sink?' Further questions can encourage interpretation, such as 'Why do you think this floats/sinks?' Allow the children time to discuss their ideas. This will enable them to see that others hold different interpretations and that there are other ways of viewing the world.

Differentiation

By support: younger children will need more interaction and support than older children. This can be achieved through questioning and adult participation. Older children can be given a focus for their exploration, such as 'Find out how you can make these floating objects sink.'

By outcome: older children will give more sophisticated interpretations of their observations, based on their experiences of water play and bath time, although they may not be scientifically accurate.

Background information

Interpretation is often a forgotten part of the scientific process. It is, however, a very important skill in science, because it is fundamental in the understanding of scientific concepts. Teachers need to provide opportunities for children to interpret their observations during the activity, and they should also help them to make sense of their interpretations and listen to others' ideas after the activity is over. Floating and sinking provides many opportunities for interpretations, particularly if care is taken in the provision of objects to explore.

Children will often develop a theory about floating and sinking at an early age: that light objects will float and heavy objects will sink. They may also think that there is a correlation between big and heavy and small and light. A cork may actually be heavier than other objects but will float because it is less dense than water. This can be explained to children as light for its size. Density is thought of as a very complex concept, but we do not believe it is too complex to begin to understand at this early stage. Indeed, an early start to understanding will be of considerable help in later years. A lump of Plasticine will sink because it is denser than water (is heavy for its size) but can be made to float by changing its shape so that there is more upthrust from the water. Aluminium foil will float but can be made to sink by squashing it up into a small ball (compressing it as much as possible), so that its density (weight for size) is greater. An orange will float but can be made to sink in two ways: by removing the peel and pith, or by leaving it in water for a while so that it absorbs the water and its density increases. A plastic bottle and a plastic beaker can be made to sink or partially sink by filling them with water. Ice balloons, water-filled balloons and air-filled balloons can be compared to see the different densities of water, ice and air. A pine cone will float but if left in the water it will close in response to the moisture and then sink. Throughout this activity it is important to encourage differing interpretations, even if they are not scientifically correct. This enables children to see that there are different ideas from those they hold, and this will challenge their thinking. It is only by having their preconceived theories challenged that children will construct new and more scientific meaning to explain their observations.

What next?

- Try to make something float that sinks, for example a ball of Plasticine, or something sink that floats, for example a sheet of aluminium foil. Try to explain what is happening?
- Attempt some other interpretations, such as 'How does a diver in a bottle work?' Squeeze the bottle and the diver will sink. Release the pressure and it will float again.
- Why is cornflour solid and liquid? (See 'Mixing things'.)
- Look around and find other things to try to explain how they work.
- Introduce more scientific language, such as density.

Other activities that will develop interpretation skills

Can you hear me? (page 74)   Flying high (page 69)
Me and my shadow (page 78)   Bath time for Archimedes (page 86)

Books/stories

Allen, P. (1982) *Who Sank the Boat?* London: Hamish Hamilton.

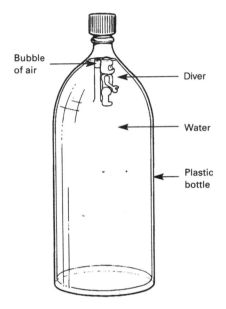

Bubble of air

Diver

Water

Plastic bottle

BODY MAPPING

Body mapping

Get a child to lie on a large piece of paper and another child to draw round her or him. This might need to have close supervision to avoid ink on clothes and to achieve a recognizable outline. Alternatively, you can draw around a child in chalk on the playground. Encourage the children to look at the outline and ask questions. What does the body outline look like? Can you tell which child it is? What parts of the body can you see? At this point encourage the children to label the parts of the body they can see and draw in any 'inside' parts that they know about.

Resources

A large surface to draw on (sheet of paper, wallpaper, opened out cardboard box, a playground).
Chalk.
Crayons or felt-tip pens.

Language

Descriptions using own words.

Names for parts of the body: arms, legs, head, shoulders, knees, toes, hands.

How it fits

With topics

Topics on ourselves

With National Curriculum

- Sc1, Developing recording skills.
- Sc2, Developing understanding of *humans as organisms*.
- Eng3, Developing writing skills.

With the Early Years Curriculum

Knowledge and understanding of the world.
Language and literacy.

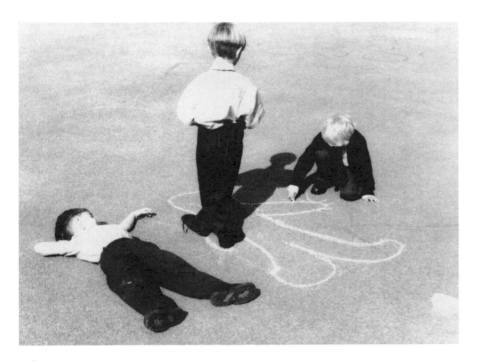

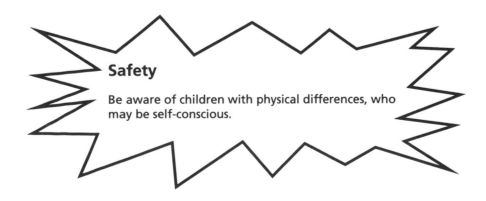

Safety

Be aware of children with physical differences, who may be self-conscious.

BODY MAPPING

Setting the scene

The focus for this activity is on the parts of the body, mainly external, but introducing some internal parts if appropriate. This can be a group or whole-class activity, with each group of children making up their own body and then presenting it to the class. You can also focus on what each part of the body does, such as joints allowing movement, toes for balance, fingers for picking up.

Developing children's learning

Language

Encourage the children to name the parts of the body using their own terms. These may be different from more scientific terms: for example, 'tummy' could be used instead of 'stomach' or 'tabs' could be used instead of 'ears'. Introduce the more acceptable terms as appropriate.

Scientific skills

This activity can help to develop recording skills. Annotated drawings in science are a good recording method and can help to assess children's understanding when used in conjunction with other techniques.

Conceptual understanding

The main focus for this activity is understanding the parts of the body and beginning to consider how they work. Young children should begin to name the external parts of the body and add internal parts where appropriate.

BODY MAPPING

Attitudes

Children are naturally curious about their bodies, and this activity is a motivating one for them. It can also help to develop respect for others and respect for our bodies.

Supporting children's learning

Most children will have no problem identifying the major parts of the body, but they may need some help thinking about the smaller bits, such as knuckles or neck, and the parts that have lots of names, such as the leg: calf, thigh, knee, ankle, shin. It is not necessary for children to know all of these, but encourage them to learn from each other and label everything they can think of. Recording the names of the parts of the body can be done individually or in groups. You could begin with a group activity on a large scale and finish with individual body shapes to label.

Children who have problems thinking what the parts of the body actually do can be helped by getting them to imagine what it would be like to be without that part of the body. What would we walk like without knees? How would we drink if we had no wrists? What would it be like if we had no neck?

Differentiation

By task: with younger children it may be best to focus on external parts of the body only. The teacher will be able to scaffold the learning through focused questions but will have a clear picture of the children's understandings through the initial body maps. Older children can be encouraged to think more about the internal workings of the body.

Background information

The main focus for this activity is the external parts of the body, although some discussion of internal parts is inevitable. There are many different parts that the children can label and discuss.

Head

The head is the location of many sensory organs, such as eyes, nose, ears, teeth, lips, hair, chin, cheek, neck. Inside the head is the brain, protected by the skull. The brain and nerves make up the central nervous system, which sends electrical impulses to control many functions, both involuntary (blinking and breathing) and voluntary (walking and jumping). The brain also interprets messages sent to it from around the body (for example, what we see or hear).

Chest

The chest houses some internal organs, such as the heart, a large muscle which is part of the circulatory system and pumps blood around the body. It also contains the lungs, which form part of the respiratory system and have a huge surface area that allows large quantities of gas to pass into and out of the blood.

BODY MAPPING

Arms

Shoulders, armpit, forearm, elbow, wrist, hand, knuckle, fingers, nails and so on can all be added to the diagram. The arm and hand allow gross and fine movement. Opposing fingers and thumb are unique to humans and apes, allow small things to be picked up and have enabled humans to make complex structures and detailed drawing and writing.

Abdomen

The children may provide names such as 'tummy' or 'tummy button'. While this is quite acceptable, you could introduce more scientific words, such as abdomen, stomach and navel. Inside the abdomen is the stomach, part of the digestive system which processes the food we eat. Food is broken up into smaller parts in the mouth and mixed with saliva. It then passes into the stomach, where it is mixed with digestive juices and broken up even more. By the time it passes into the small intestine it has become very liquid. In the small intestine the nutrients are absorbed into the blood through the wall of the intestine, and in the large intestine more liquid is absorbed, so that the excreted remains are fairly solid undigested food, which passes out of the anus, or 'bottom' as children may call it.

The abdomen also houses the liver, which is the chemical factory of the blood, and the kidneys, which are part of the urinary system and act as filters separating out the blood and toxins. Toxins in a diluted form are stored in the bladder and flushed out of the body in urine.

Legs

Thighs, knees, calf, shin, ankles, toes and ball of foot are all parts of the legs and provide mobility.

What next?

- Shapes of the internal parts of the body can be cut out of coloured card and the children can be encouraged to place them appropriately on the body outline.
- Examine a collection of bones or try to reconstruct skeletons, depending on resources available. What bones belong where? What bones do you have in your body? What bones can you feel?

Other activities that will develop knowledge and understanding of humans as organisms

You and me (page 45)   Me and my shadow (page 78)

Books/stories

Arnold, T. (1998) *I'm Falling to Bits*. Hove: McDonald Young.
Barner, B. (1997) *Dem Bones*. Harmondsworth: Puffin.
Smallman, C. (1986) *Outside in*. London: Macdonald.

BODY MAPPING

Computer program

Body Mapper, produced by Invicta Software.

Poems

Flowers grow like this
Trees grow like this
I grow
Just like that.

Songs

Head Shoulders Knees and Toes.
One Finger One Thumb Keep Moving.

SORTING PLANTS

What before?

Experience of having plants in the classroom.

Resources

A collection of pot plants and/or plants in the garden, park etc.

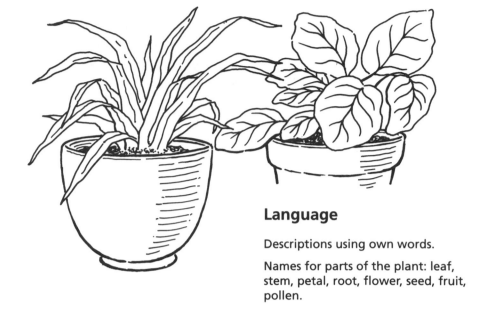

Language

Descriptions using own words.

Names for parts of the plant: leaf, stem, petal, root, flower, seed, fruit, pollen.

Sorting plants

Give the children one plant to observe closely, noting all the different parts of the plant. Encourage them to identify the different parts of the plant and introduce the correct terms as appropriate. Then give the children a collection of plants to observe and ask them to note the similarities and differences between them. Encourage them to describe in their own words what they see and what the similarities and differences are. Ask the children to sort the plants into groups according to their own criteria or criteria suggested by you, such as colour of leaves, size of plants, shape of leaves, number of leaves.

How it fits

With topics

Topics on the environment and living and growing.

With National Curriculum

- Sc1, Developing observational skills.
- Sc1, Developing classificatory skills.
- Sc2, Developing understanding of *green plants as organisms* and the *classification of plants*.
- Eng1, Developing language skills.
- Ma, Developing number skills.
- Ma, Developing understanding of shape and size.
- Art, Developing appreciation for colour and pattern in plants.

With the Early Years Curriculum

Knowledge and understanding of the world.
Language and literacy.
Mathematics.
Creative development.

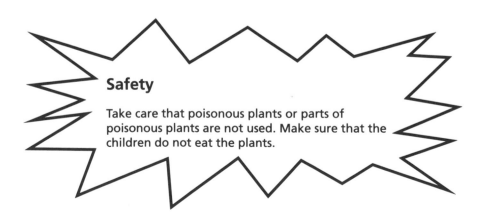

Safety

Take care that poisonous plants or parts of poisonous plants are not used. Make sure that the children do not eat the plants.

SORTING PLANTS

Setting the scene

The focus for this activity is developing understanding of the similarities and differences between plants. This can be child-led, with children identifying similarities or differences as observed by them.

Developing children's learning

Language

Children should be encouraged to observe for themselves and to describe plants using their own words. This could form part of a game where children can describe their chosen plant and others can guess from the description. Children should also be encouraged to name the parts of plants, such as leaf, stem, root, flower, petal.

Mathematics

Children can compare size and shape of leaves or the number of leaves, shoots or flowers on a plant.

Scientific skills

This activity can help to develop classificatory skills, which are an important part of the scientific process and involved in the development of many other scientific conceptual areas: for example, sorting and classifying materials according to their properties (see 'Dressing teddy'). Classification begins from observation, so observational skills are also enhanced through a classificatory activity.

Conceptual understanding

The main focus for this activity is observing and classification of plants according to observable features, such as colour or shape. Children should also be able to name the external parts of plants.

SORTING PLANTS

Attitudes

This activity will help to develop curiosity and attention to detail, both of which are important scientific attitudes, necessary for future exploration and investigation.

Art

The pattern of the leaves can be compared. This can be seen well by leaf printing, which will also help children to consider the different shapes and sizes. The colour of plants can be compared with the colours on paint colour charts, obtainable from DIY stores. This will help children to see that there are many shades of colours such as green (also see 'Observing around us').

Supporting children's learning

Children should be encouraged to look closely at one plant and draw what they see. Features of the plants can be pointed out to the children to help them with their observations and drawings. Ask the children to compare a collection of plants with their plant and to look for similarities and differences between them. Again, the teacher can be a good role model here in sharing the observations with the children. Encourage the children to group the plants according to observable features. There may be similar patterns in the leaves or flowers or different numbers of leaves or shape of leaves. Discuss the sets of plants with the children and encourage them to say why each plant is in a particular set. Ask the children if they can re-sort the plants into different groups according to other observable criteria.

Differentiation

By task: there can be a move with age from grouping plants based on simple observable features to classifying plants based on a number of criteria. The older and most able children could begin to undertake some simple identification based on the observable features.

Background information

It is necessary for children to be aware of similarities and differences between groups of objects and even events. Much of science at this stage is concerned with the recognition of similarities and differences. For example, children should be aware of the similarities and differences between themselves and others, plants and animals and different materials. It is also necessary to recognize similarities and differences to be able to identify different variables in an investigation. Therefore, classification is a skill which is a prerequisite to further skills necessary in scientific exploration and investigation: that is, fair testing and handling variables. The ability to classify develops with age and experience and children begin to move from sorting using one very simple criterion, such as size or colour, to recognition of more complex criteria, such as number of leaves, shape of leaves or type of flower. Later, children should be able to assign plants to groups according to features and then re-sort

SORTING PLANTS

according to different criteria. When children are able to separate a plant because of a number of different features they can use the skill of classification to identify different plants.

There are a number of different features in a group of plants which may be useful to identify. Most green, flowering plants have certain features in common, such as leaves, flowers, roots and stems, although there will be differences in fine detail. For example, the upper side of leaves will usually be darker in colour than the underside, and the parts inside the flower may look very different. Plants are different because they are adapted for particular environments and situations. If the plant usually grows in shady places, the leaves may be large and darker green to capture as much light as possible. If it grows in a dry place it may have small, thin, dry leaves to prevent water loss or have succulent leaves which store water. The way that plants reproduce by runners, as with the strawberry plant and spider plant, or by dropping their leaves to the ground, as with the umbrella plant, can also provide an interesting comparison. These features can often be seen in a collection of house plants and can lead to further discussion about differences in flower shape, pollination and germination.

What next?

- Make close observational drawings of plants.
- Make a classification tree or classification key to identify the plants.
- Play some identification games. Try to guess a chosen plant by asking questions about it.
- Grow a plant from a cutting or a seed. Beans, sunflower seeds and cress will all grow well from seed. Spider plants, umbrella plants and geraniums will grow well from cuttings.

Other activity that will develop knowledge and understanding of green plants as organisms

Observing around us (page 40)

Other activities that will develop the skill of classification

You and me (page 45)
Dressing teddy (page 54)

Sticky glues (page 64)
How does it work? (page 82)

Books/stories

Briggs, R. (1970) *Jim and the Beanstalk*. Harmondsworth: Puffin.
Hodgson Burnett, F. (1971) *The Secret Garden*. London: Heinemann.

Songs

In an English Country Garden.
Oats and Beans and Barley Grow.

OBSERVING AROUND US

What before?

Experiences of looking around school and of observing the world around them.

Observing around us

Take the children out into their local environment to observe their surroundings using all their senses. Tell them to close their eyes and to listen very carefully to all the sounds they can hear. Ask the children to tell you what they can hear.

Ask them to close their eyes again and to take a deep breath and smell all the different smells. Blindfold a 'volunteer' child and lead her or him, indirectly, to a tree, bush or wall and ask her or him to feel their surroundings. Lead the child back to the starting point, remove the blindfold and see if she or he can find the tree, bush or wall. Use the paint colour charts to see how many different colours the children can find in the environment. See what different animals and plants you can find in the local environment and note where they live.

Safety

This activity works better if there are a number of supervising adults, so that children are carefully supervised. Check the area you are working in to make sure there are no unsafe objects. Children should also be well briefed about staying with their adult supervisor, not using their sense of taste and not picking flowers or plants or mishandling minibeasts.

Resources

The local environment (playground, yard, field, park, street).
Some paint colour charts from the local DIY shop.
Blindfolds.

Language

Leaf.
Flower.
Plant.
Soil.
Minibeast.
Live.

How it fits

With topics

Topics on the environment, living and growing and minibeasts

With National Curriculum

- Sc1, Developing observational skills.
- Sc2, Developing understanding of *life processes* and *living things in their environment*.
- Eng1, Developing language skills.
- Geog, Developing understanding of the local surroundings.
- Art, Developing appreciation of colour and pattern in the environment.

With the Early Years Curriculum

Knowledge and understanding of the world.
Language and literacy.
Creative development.

OBSERVING AROUND US

Setting the scene

The children may be very familiar with their local environment, but they may have overlooked many aspects and will probably not have looked closely at animal and plant habitats or the variety of shades of colour in the environment. The focus for this activity is observation within the environment. Encourage them to use all their senses in their observations, to look for patterns in the environment and to observe similarities and differences between things they see in the environment.

Developing children's learning

Language

Allow the children to describe their observations in their own words. Encourage them to name the things they see and add words where appropriate (for example, plant, flower, seed, red, green, worm, spider).

Scientific skills

This is a good activity to help to develop observational skills. Remember that observations do not always have to be 'scientific', and are in part personal and creative. See 'I-spy ice balloons' for more information on developing and supporting the development of observational skills.

Conceptual understanding

The main focus for this activity is the conceptual understanding of the relationship between plants and animals in the local environment. Children can look for evidence of plants and animals living in the locality, identify and name them and then consider the interrelationships between them.

Attitudes

This activity is useful for developing curiosity about the familiar world, patience when looking closely at small plants and animals and respect for living things.

Geography

Children should be able to observe and explore the physical and human features of their locality. They should be able to consider the effect of human activity on the plants and animals living in the local environment.

Art

Children should be able to observe and appreciate the variety of colour, pattern and texture in their local environment. This can include colour of foliage, brickwork and stones, pattern in nature and construction, and the texture of leaves, soil and stones.

OBSERVING AROUND US

Supporting children's learning

Children can be helped to observe their environment in a variety of ways.

- Focusing on one sense at a time. Allow them time to listen, smell and touch things in the environment.
- Ask the children questions about their observations. For example, 'What can you hear when your eyes are closed?', 'What do you think this feels like?'
- Be a good role model for the children, observing and showing enthusiasm for things found.
- When listening to sounds in the environment, you could ask children to name loud sounds and quiet sounds or sounds made by people and natural sounds.
- Use paint colour charts to help children to recognize colour in the environment. Give them a chart each and ask them to find one thing that matches each colour. This is quite creative, as the colours often have interesting names.
- When looking at plants and animals in the environment, questions could focus on the similarities and differences between the living things and their habitats. 'Where does the worm live?', 'Does the spider live near the worm?', 'How is this plant/minibeast different?'

Differentiation

By task: young children can be given a colour chart with distinctly different colours to match, while older children could use a chart with different shades of colour on to aid their identification.

By support: younger children will need more supervision and support when observing minibeasts. They need help to see small things and to ensure they do not touch inappropriately.

Background information

Observation is a complex skill and is described fully in 'I-spy ice balloons'. The main focus for this activity is observations of the complexity of life in the local environment. Every environment, whether urban, suburban or rural, whether a park or hard core playground, is teeming with life and colour. Sound, smells, colours and so on will vary from environment to environment and from season to season or even day to day. There is always a lot to observe. You may hear cars, voices, animals (birds, dogs), the rustle of leaves or the wind whistling around a building. You may smell damp soil, rain in the air, cars or hot tarmac. You can feel the texture of trees with different bark patterns or the different surfaces of a building. You may feel the wind or sun on your face or the scrunch of dead leaves underfoot. Feeling a tree with your eyes closed focuses your attention on the feel of the bark, how wide the tree is, whether there are any characteristic bumps or shapes and what the ground around the tree feels like. When you have to find the tree again you can only use the non-visual clues to help you. You will also find many patterns within the environment, on the bark of trees, on bricks, grates, walls etc. There are many different shades of colour in the environment and we do not always appreciate this when looking around us. The paint colour charts encourage children to look closely for unusual colours or shades of colour in their local environment, and are a good way of increasing appreciation of the complexity of colour in nature.

Regardless of the locality, there will be plenty of different things to observe and find. Minibeasts will live in cracks in pavements and bricks, as well as in soil, on plants and in trees. It is probably best to name the small animals you find 'minibeasts', as that is an acceptable term encompassing all arachnids, insects, crustaceans and so on that you will find. You may wish to give children more specific names as well, such as spider, fly or woodlouse. Plants will grow in crevices in bricks or walls, and lichens will even grow on the pavement or bricks and walls themselves. A tree is a good ecological niche in itself. You might find smaller plants, such as ferns and mosses, growing on it, shrubs growing under its protective foliage and many different animals living in and on the tree. You can use an umbrella to collect minibeasts from foliage. Hook the umbrella over a branch and shake the branch so that small animals fall into the open umbrella. The soil around the tree may be different from the surrounding soil because of the leaf litter from the tree, and there will be animals living in and around the soil and leaf litter. The patterns made by the sun shining through the tree's foliage can be observed, as can the noise made by the wind rustling through the tree. The bark of the tree will have a distinctive pattern: this can be felt and bark rubbings can be made so that the patterns can be more closely observed. The colours of the bark, old and new leaves can be observed and compared to other colours in the environment. If you are not lucky enough to have a nearby tree then look at and around the school buildings. You will probably find plants growing around the foundations, lichens on the stones and pavement areas and minibeasts living in the cracks and crevices. You can observe the patterns and colours of the building materials. Rubbings can be made of grates and bricks and close observational drawings made of plants or animals without moving them.

What next?

- Collect animals found in the environment to keep for a few days and observe. Worms, snails and woodlice are particularly useful to keep for a short time in the classroom.
- Make close observational drawings of plants and animals found.
- Sort plants or animals found (see 'Sorting plants').
- Look specifically for pattern in the environment by comparing bark, grate or brick rubbings.
- Observe the same environment at a different time of year. This could be a tree, which could be observed each season to see the seasonal changes.
- Observe a different environment and compare it with your own.
- Mount small objects, such as leaf skeletons, dead insect wings or feathers, and use a slide projector to view them. This will help to enhance observations.

Other activities that involve life processes and living things in their environment

Sorting plants (page 36)   I-spy ice balloons (page 8)
Recording weather (page 22)

OBSERVING AROUND US

Books/stories

Carle, E. (1970) *The Hungry Caterpillar*. Harmondsworth: Puffin.
Carle, E. (1974) *The Bad Tempered Ladybird*. Harmondsworth: Penguin.
Carle, E. (1987) *The Tiny Seed*. Harmondsworth: Puffin/Hamish Hamilton.
Vernon, J. (1974) *Mr Mead and His Garden*. London: Jonathan Cape.

Nursery rhymes

Mary, Mary Quite Contrary.
Incy Wincy Spider.

Poem

There was a little grasshopper
That was always on the jump
And because he never looked ahead
He always got a bump.

YOU AND ME

Resources

Pens.
Paper.
Mirrors.

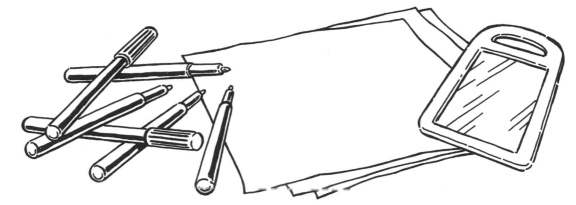

You and me

Allow children to look at themselves and others and to note similarities and differences. Allow them to describe what they see and what the similarities and differences are between themselves and others. Children can group the class according to observable features, gender, eye colour, hair colour etc. Children can record their observations in drawings, identikit pictures or pictograms.

Language

Descriptions using own words

Names for parts of the body: tongue, hands, hair, eyes, toes.
Similar/different.
Like/unlike.

How it fits

With topics

Topics on ourselves and living and growing.

With National Curriculum

- Sc1, Developing observational skills.
- Sc1, Developing the skill of classification.
- Sc1, Developing the skill of recording and communicating.
- Sc2, Developing understanding of *humans as organisms*.
- Eng1, Developing language skills.
- Ma, Developing skills of measuring height, hand spans and weight.

With the Early Years Curriculum

Knowledge and understanding of the world.
Language and literacy.

Safety

Be aware of children who may not live with their genetic family. Be sensitive to feelings about appearance, both 'racially' and personally. The use of colour charts to look at finer detail, such as eye and hair colour, could prevent unwelcome comparison.

YOU AND ME

Setting the scene

This activity can initially be child-led and then focused by the teacher. Children can notice similarities and differences between them and a partner, and this can be used to make a class profile. Use a mirror to help children to look closely at their own features. The teacher, being socially aware of the class, can then set a task of mapping these features out. Which hair and eye colours go together? Who can roll their tongue?

Developing children's learning

Language

Encourage the children to use their own words to describe themselves and their peers. Focus on shape, colour and names of parts of the body, such as tongue, ears, hair and eyes, as these are parts which have characteristics that are genetically inherited.

Scientific skills

This is another activity which would help to develop observational skills. See 'I-spy ice balloons', for more information. Encourage the children to look closely and match colours, shapes, characteristics etc.

Scientific conceptual understanding

This is the main focus of this activity: that is, the similarities and differences between humans. Focus on the characteristics of different parts of the human body, particularly those features that are genetically linked, such as hair and eye colour, right or left handedness, ability to roll your tongue and whether ear lobes are attached or free.

Attitudes

This activity is a good one to develop curiosity and attention to detail, but it is also a good vehicle for developing respect for others. Ensure that the children do not make fun of any differences observed in others. In situations where you have children from different cultural or ethnic backgrounds, you might wish to focus on the similarities rather than the differences. Do not overemphasize family differences, especially where children may not be living with genetic families or where the family has only one parent.

Mathematics

There are a number of opportunities to measure within this activity. Height, weight, head circumference, hand span and foot size can all be measured. Sensitivity will be needed if some children are overweight or have growth difficulties, and in such cases it may be better to focus on other measurements that will cause less concern.

Supporting children's learning

Encourage the children to look closely at their own facial features in a mirror and to compare their features with the person sitting next to them. Some children will feel uncomfortable comparing themselves with others, but if handled sensitively, concentrating on neutral features, this can be overcome. It could be a good plenary activity to have the children say what they like about the way they look, or what their favourite thing is that they can do. This provides scope for the children to show what makes them individual, be it tongue rolling or preference for a colour or a television programme. You can ask children to produce a passport or profile all about themselves, which can celebrate themselves as unique individuals. They can look at a variety of features and characteristics, such as:

- age;
- gender;
- height;
- hair colour;
- curly/wavy/straight hair;
- hair length;
- eye colour;
- head circumference;
- weight;
- hand span;
- preferred hand;
- whether they can roll their tongue;
- foot size;
- favourite colour;
- favourite television programme.

Pictograms of eye colour or hair colour or other features can be made or close observational drawing and identikit pictures which will help to focus on specific features such as eye shapes etc.

Differentiation

By Task: with the very youngest children it will be enough to concentrate on physical details such as eye colour, hair colour, rolling tongues and ear lobes.

Older children can observe more features and begin to explore the features they share with other children and family members.

By support: younger children will need support to be able to make observations and take measurements. Older children will be able to undertake the work with less support from the teacher or adult helpers.

Background information

Most physical features are genetically transmitted, with half your genetic information coming from the maternal side and half from the paternal side. The genetic information is passed from parents to offspring through genes which are located on the chromosomes in each cell of your body. Every person has 46 chromosomes, which are found in pairs. One of each pair comes from your mother and one from your father, so each parent gives 23 chromosomes to a child. As a result of this complex exchange of genetic information everyone is genetically unique, apart from identical brothers or sisters. Identical twins share genetic information because each twin has developed from one divided cell containing genetic information from both parents. Eye colour is one of the most obvious characteristics that is directly inherited from the parents. Some physical traits, such as ability to roll the tongue or whether the big toe is longer than the second toe, are less obvious.

Genetic traits you may think of include:

- Ability to roll the tongue.
- Whether the ear lobes are attached or loose.
- Shape of the face (children can draw around their faces in a mirror with an OHT pen). Is the face round, square, oval, heart-shaped?
- Colour of eyes (brown, blue, grey, hazel, green, black).
- Colour of hair (blond, brown, black, grey, white).
- Whether the hair is curly or straight.
- Which toe is the longest.
- Whether you are right or left handed.
- Shape of the hairline (peaked, square, round).

Some of these traits are dominant, such as brown eyes, right handed, loose ear lobes, long eye lashes. Other traits are a mix of genetic information from both parents, such as height, weight and to some extent hair colour. Some characteristics are not genetic, such as accent, likings for food or birth marks. Some characteristics can 'skip' a generation or two before emerging again. This means they have been passed down through the generations but not emerged because of more dominant characteristics. Some features are cultural, such as the prevalence of red hair to the north of Britain, or the blondness of Scandinavians.

What next?

- Observe family traits. You could use your own family or the royal family as an example. This would prevent any concerns if there were children who did not know their biological parents.
- Map out a family tree. Other families could be used here as exemplars.

- Compare skin colour or eye colour using paint colour charts (obtainable from DIY stores).
- Make an individual classification profile or a book about 'Me'. This can be done using a computer database. Information for all children in the class can be compiled to make a class book or computer database or spreadsheet.
- Play identification games. Choose one member of the class, and the children have to guess who it is from your description.
- Looking at animal family trees.
- Looking at cultural differences between people.

Other activity that will develop knowledge and understanding of humans as organisms

Body mapping (page 31)

Other activities that will develop the skill of classification

Sorting plants (page 36)
Dressing teddy (page 54)

Sticky glues (page 64)
How does it work? (page 82)

Books/stories

Ahlberg, A. (1981) *Peepo*. Harmondsworth: Puffin.
Pearse, P. (1988) *See How You Grow*. London: Macdonald.

Game

Guess Who? (Waddington).

BAKING CHANGES

What before?

Pre-school baking experience. Mixing materials, e.g. sand and water.

Resources

Recipe for chocolate mini muffins.
150 grams plain flour.
Two level tablespoons of cocoa powder.
One level dessertspoon of baking powder.
One-quarter teaspoon salt.
One large egg, lightly beaten.
40 grams caster sugar.
120 millilitres of milk.
50 grams of butter, melted and cooled slightly.
50 grams of plain chocolate drops.
For the topping: 65 grams of plain chocolate drops.
Two whole mini muffin tins, well greased.
Two mixing bowls.
Large spoons.
Pan.
Sieve.
Oven.

Language

Descriptions using own words.
Names for ingredients.
Process words, such as: melting, stirring, folding, sieving, cooling, simmering, solidifying.
Measuring words, such as: weigh, gram, millilitre.

Baking changes

Talk through the recipe with the children. Make sure all the resources are ready, the children's hands are clean and they are wearing aprons. Allow the children to weigh the ingredients and to mix them together following the recipe. Make sure you allow them opportunities to observe the different ingredients and encourage the children to use their own words to describe them. Encourage them to predict what will happen when different materials are mixed together. Allow them to compare their predictions with what actually happens. Introduce more scientific words, such as melt, solidify, solid, liquid.

How it fits

With topics

Topics on food, cooking, materials and celebrations.

With National Curriculum

- Sc1, Developing observational skills.
- Sc1, Developing prediction skills.
- Sc3, Developing understanding of *how materials change when mixed or heated*.
- Eng1, Developing language skills.
- Eng2, Developing reading skills.
- Ma, Developing skills in measuring.

With the Early Years Curriculum

Knowledge and understanding of the world.
Language and literacy.
Mathematics.

Safety

Careful supervision is needed at all times during this activity. Take special care with kitchen implements, which may be broken or sharp, and with hot ovens. Take care as well to ensure that the children are aware of the importance of hygiene, and be aware of any food allergies a child may have.

BAKING CHANGES

Setting the scene

Many children have enjoyed baking activities at home and in nurseries, play groups or schools. However, this activity differs from these experiences because the focus is on the materials and how they change during the mixing and baking process. It is a small group activity, which needs the careful supervision of an adult helper. It is important that you share the learning objectives with the adult helper and discuss, prior to the activity, questions that would promote learning about materials and how they change (see below).

When you talk through the recipe with the children, take time to look at all the ingredients and encourage the children to describe them using their own words. You can introduce more scientific words at this stage by describing something which is wet as liquid or encourage close observation by comparing similar materials such as salt and sugar.

Developing children's learning

Language

Encourage the children to describe the process changes that occur in baking using their own words.

Scientific skills

This activity is a good vehicle to develop observational skills and the skill of prediction. Encourage the children to look closely at how the different ingredients mix together and predict what will happen when another ingredient is added or the mixture is cooked.

Scientific conceptual understanding

The main focus of this activity is the changes that occur when different substances are mixed, heated or cooled. Encourage the children to look closely during the baking process and observe changes.

Mathematics

During the activity the children will be weighing and measuring the ingredients. The use of standard measures in baking can be discussed, as can the effect of different temperatures on baking.

BAKING CHANGES

Attitudes

This activity will help to develop curiosity in children. It will help them to look at a familiar process in more detail or in a slightly different way. It will also help the children to be methodical, which is necessary later in scientific development.

Supporting children's learning

- Asking questions to encourage observation: 'How is the salt different from the sugar?'
- Asking questions to encourage prediction: 'What do you think will happen when we mix the egg, milk and melted butter?'
- Asking questions to focus on the material change: 'How has the mixture changed after baking?'

Differentiation

By task: with younger children the task should be very oral and practical. Older children will be able to read the recipe and can follow up the work with written descriptions of the changes observed.

By support: younger children will require help to weigh and measure. They may need the ingredients weighed out for them, and need to be shown the technique of mixing etc. Older children can undertake weighing and measuring for themselves.

By outcome: older children will be able to use more scientific words to describe what happens to the ingredients on mixing and heating.

Background information

Recipe for chocolate mini muffins

Pre-heat the oven to gas mark 6, 400 °F, 200 °C.

Sift the flour, cocoa powder and salt into a large bowl. *Note how the lumps are removed by sifting and the powders seem finer.*

In a separate bowl mix together the egg, sugar, milk and melted butter. *Note that the sugar begins to dissolve in the liquid and the butter mixes loosely with the milk.*

Sieve all the dry ingredients again straight on to the egg mixture.

With a large spoon mix the dry ingredients slowly, but don't beat or stir. *Note how the two mixtures combine and how the resulting mixture has changed. The mixture will be lumpy and uneven.*

Fold the chocolate drops into the mixture. Don't over-mix. *Note that the chocolate drops do not really mix into the mixture but keep their shape.*

Put the mixture into the muffin tin and bake for 10 minutes on a high shelf in the oven. Cool in the tin for about 5 minutes before putting the muffins on to a cooling tray. *Note how the mixture has expanded, how the texture has changed and how the chocolate drops have melted a little into the mixture.*

While the muffins are cooling make the topping by melting the remaining chocolate drops in a bowl over a pan of simmering water. *Observe the changes in the chocolate drops as they melt in the pan.*

When the muffins are cool spoon a little melted chocolate on to each one and leave to cool. *Note how the chocolate topping changes as it cools and solidifies.*

What next?

- Draw cartoon pictures of the activity. This will help to sequence the activity and develop the skill of recording and communicating.
- Try some other baking activities in which changes to materials occur, e.g. baking bread, cooking an egg, making butter out of cream by shaking in a jar, or making jelly.
- Older children can look at whether baking and cooking changes are reversible or not.
- Try writing out your recipe.

Other activities that will develop understanding of how materials change when mixed or heated

Mixing things (page 18)   Sticky glues (page 64)

Books/stories

Fowler, R. (1987) *Cat's Cake*. Cambridge: Piccadilly Press.
Green, M. (1978) *Mr Bembleman's Bakery*. New York: Parents Magazine Press.

Songs

Pat-a-cake.
Hot Cross Buns (one a penny, two a penny).
Let's Bake a Cake.

DRESSING TEDDY

What before?

Experience of dressing-up.

Resources

Large teddy or doll.
Doll's clothes, old baby clothes
or pieces of material.

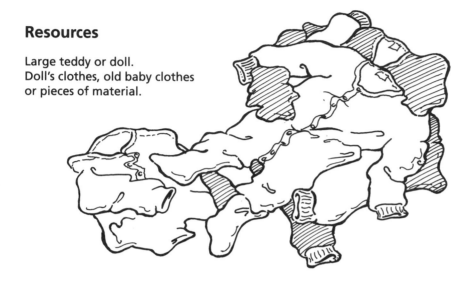

Dressing teddy

Give a group of children a set of clothes and ask them to pick out outfits to dress teddy in for various weathers or seasons. Ask them to justify their choices and compare these with what other groups have chosen. Ask the children to identify why some materials will keep teddy warm or dry.

Language

Descriptions using own words:
warm, hot, cold, wet, rain, sun.

Other weather words.

Soft.
Smooth.
Plastic.
Wool.

Other material texture words.

How it fits

With topics

Topics on ourselves and weather.

With National Curriculum

- Sc1, Developing observational skills.
- Sc1, Developing classification skills.
- Sc3, Developing understanding of the *properties of materials and how materials can be grouped together*.
- Eng1, Developing language skills.

With the Early Years Curriculum

Knowledge and understanding of the world.
Language and literacy.

Safety

Be aware that some plastic materials are not breathable and may pose a suffocation risk.

DRESSING TEDDY

Setting the scene

The focus for this activity is on the properties of materials. Before the children get to decide how to dress teddy encourage them to look at the materials closely and to think about what they wear in different weathers. The activity can take place in a carpeted area, a home corner or sitting at a small table. It will complement other activities that look more formally at different fabrics and their properties.

Developing children's learning

Language

Encourage the children to describe the clothes using their own words. More scientific words can be introduced to extend the children's vocabulary as appropriate. Words or phrases describing the weave of the material can also be used.

Scientific skills

Encourage the children to observe the textures and qualities of the different materials. By asking them to sort the clothes into ones which teddy will wear in different weather conditions, you will be encouraging them to classify the material into properties suitable for different weather conditions.

Scientific conceptual understanding

The focus of the activity is the properties of the material to keep teddy dry, warm, cool and so on, in each weather condition. This will focus on the insulation, waterproof and absorbent properties of different materials.

Attitudes

This activity will help to develop enthusiasm and curiosity in children, by looking at the familiar in a different way.

Supporting children's learning

Most children will not have any difficulty picking out suitable clothes, though they may choose their own criteria for picking, such as colour or personal preference. Encourage them to think of whether teddy would be warm or cold in the material rather than what looks good or fits well.

If you want to encourage closer observation of the materials, having hand lenses available will focus the children's attention on texture and weave. This can lead to discussion on the effects of different texture and weave and can be supported by questioning. Are the materials closely woven? How do they feel? How fluffy or thin is the material?

The children should also be encouraged to consider why they made particular choices. They could consider who chooses their clothes, what influences choices and why they are wearing particular choices of clothes.

DRESSING TEDDY

The activity can be an independent or small group activity that can occur as part of directed play. The teacher's role in developing understanding is in setting the activity and discussing ideas with children. The children can be asked to sort all teddy's clothes into ones to wear in winter or summer, when raining or sunny and hot, or to dress Teddy for a cold day or wet day. It is important to keep the number of variables small, so it is advisable to use a maximum of two types of weather conditions at any one time. It is also important to find time to talk to the children about their choices, and this can take place on the carpet at the end of a session or day. This discussion time will allow the children to express their ideas, to consolidate their own understandings from observations, to listen to the ideas of others and to develop new ideas as a result.

Differentiation

By task: younger children can dress teddy appropriately for a particular weather condition. Older children can sort the clothes according to one or two simple criteria (wet, dry; summer, winter).

Background information

If fabrics are observed through a hand lens the different construction can be seen. Woven fabrics have intertwined threads, while knitted fabrics have threads that are looped together and some fabrics, such as felt, are made by compressing material together. Small pieces of fabric can be put into slide binders and projected on to a wall or screen, using a slide projector. This will show even more detail of the structure of the fabric.

Fabric insulation properties depend on the weave of the material. In most fabrics the material is surrounded by holes, which trap air and help insulation. A fabric with a fluffy side will trap a layer of air next to the skin, which also acts as insulation. Thin, loosely woven material will allow air to circulate and so cool the skin. The insulation properties of different fabrics can be explored by wrapping cups of warm water or a small hot water bottle in different fabrics and seeing how long it takes for the water to cool. Try using iced water or ice cubes as children often believe that fabrics that are good insulators keep things warm but not cold.

The weave of different fabrics will also determine strength, as loosely woven or knitted fabric may tend to fray. Some loosely woven fabrics are also prone to shrinkage if not washed correctly. This may occur if the fibres are stretched, as with wool when spun and when loosely knitted. Washing labels in clothes give indications of the washing needs and whether special care is needed, and tests can be made on different fabrics to see how well they wash.

Some fabrics will be more absorbent than others because of the structure of the material's molecules. Water may also get trapped in the holes between threads. Materials that have been waterproofed often have a plastic or wax coating, which seals any gaps in the weave and prevents the fabric absorbing any water. Fabric can be tested for waterproofness and then sealed with a wax crayon and tested again.

What next?

- Older children may like to do more testing of fabric samples to test their suitability to perform different functions, such as keeping cool, keeping warm and keeping dry.
- Make a waterproof hat for teddy.
- Try different ways to waterproof material.
- Look closely at the weave of materials and do some drawings to show the textures.
- Look at a range of paper towels and find differences. Test the towels for strength or absorbency.

Other activities that will develop understanding of the properties of materials and how materials can be grouped together

Funny fruit (page 58)   Sticky glues (page 64)
Baking changes (page 50)

Other activities that will develop the skill of classification

Sorting plants (page 36)   How does it work? (page 82)
You and me (page 45)   Funny fruit (page 58)

Books/stories

Mr Benn books by David McKee.
The Emperor's New Clothes.

Song

This Is the Way We Dress Ourselves on a Cold and Frosty Morning.

FUNNY FRUIT

What before?

Experiences of tasting and smelling different fruits.

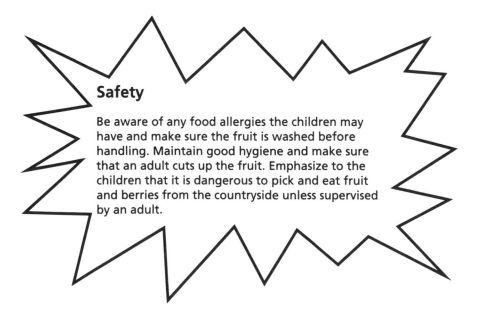

Funny fruit

Set out a range of fruit on a table. It doesn't matter which fruit you use, but choose a good range. First let the children look closely at the fruit, noting similarities and differences between the colours and shapes. Encourage the children to sort the fruit into groups according to observable features. You can also record this activity through close observational drawings and tables or Venn diagrams of groupings made.

Safety

Be aware of any food allergies the children may have and make sure the fruit is washed before handling. Maintain good hygiene and make sure that an adult cuts up the fruit. Emphasize to the children that it is dangerous to pick and eat fruit and berries from the countryside unless supervised by an adult.

Resources

A selection of fruit. For example, kiwi, apple, orange, grapes, peach, raspberry, strawberry, banana, pear, plum, lemon, lime, redcurrants, satsuma, pomegranate.
Blindfolds.

Language

Words related to the texture of fruit: rough, smooth, shiny, lumpy, soft, hard, waxy, furry.
Colours.
Patterns, e.g. speckled, veined, striped, mottled.
Tastes, e.g. bitter, sweet, tart, tangy, sour.
Parts of fruit, e.g. pip, rind, skin, pith, peel, flesh, segment, core, kernel, stone, stalk.
Smells, e.g. flowery, lemony.

How it fits

With topics

Topics on the environment and living and growing.

With National Curriculum

- Sc1, Developing observational skill.
- Sc1, Developing the skill of recording and communicating.
- Sc2, Developing understanding of *the different properties of fruits*.
- Eng1, Developing language skills.
- Art, Developing appreciation of colour and pattern in nature.

With the Early Years Curriculum

Knowledge and understanding of the world.
Language and literacy.
Creative development.

FUNNY FRUIT

Setting the scene

The children may be very familiar with some fruit but the range they have experienced may be limited, and they may have overlooked many aspects. For example, it is probable that they will not have looked closely at the insides, or the textures and colours of the fruit. The focus for this activity is the different properties of the fruit and how they can best be described and then grouped. Encourage them to use all their senses in their observations, to look for patterns in the fruit and to observe similarities and differences between things they see. This activity needs a supervising adult to help to focus the children on one aspect at a time and to assist with grouping the fruit. Records of the groupings can be made if required, either pictorially or in written or tabulated forms. Before this activity it is a good idea to display the fruit for the whole class to look at and identify. It is not important that everyone knows the names of all the fruit, because it is most important that they can see the attributes of the fruit. Slicing the fruit will often provide a new perspective, especially if it is not sliced in the usual way. For example, not many children will have seen a banana sliced in half with its skin still on, or an apple sliced in half horizontally. Try to think of different ways to slice the fruit or do unusual things like peeling a grape or peach. The more unusual the fruit, the more fun can be had, as the children's curiosity will be sparked.

Developing children's learning

Language

Encourage the children to describe their observations in their own words, introducing new words as appropriate. Encourage children to name the different parts of the fruit: for example, skin, seed or pip, flesh.

Scientific skills

This activity is good to help develop observational skills (see 'I-spy ice balloons') and the skill of classification (see 'Sorting plants'). Encourage the children to make observations of the fruit and to articulate their observations to others. Encourage the children to sort the fruit into groups according to observable features, such as colour, shape or taste. Ask them to re-sort the fruit according to other features. The activity will also develop the skills of recording and communicating. The children can record details of their observations through drawings. They can also record their groupings in a variety of different ways, either pictorially or in tables or Venn diagrams.

Scientific conceptual understanding

The main focus for this activity is the understanding of different properties of the fruit. This could be the size of the fruit or seed, the colour, the texture of the skin or flesh or the taste of the fruit. The fruit can be grouped according to these features and the groups recorded as described above.

FUNNY FRUIT

Attitudes

This activity can enthuse children, as they like to taste different fruit. It is also a useful activity to develop curiosity in children.

Art

This activity can help children to develop appreciation of colour and pattern in different fruit. Comparisons of colours and paint colour charts can be useful, and printing with some fruit can highlight interesting patterns. Citrus fruits, star fruit or an apple cut across the middle to reveal the star shape inside are good for this.

Supporting children's learning

Children can be helped to observe the whole, uncut fruit closely by focusing on one sense at a time. They can look at the fruit and compare the different colours. Using paint colour charts (available from DIY stores) is a good way to help children to recognize colour in the fruit. The texture of the fruit can be felt and the children can be encouraged to identify if the fruit is hard or soft, waxy, wet, sticky etc. The fruit can be smelt and the children can describe what it smells like. The teacher's role in this should be one of motivating and facilitating by questioning and by example. An enthusiastic interaction which asks the children to describe what they observe and which provides good examples of observation is likely to facilitate involvement and understanding in the children. At this stage the children can be encouraged to group the fruit according to one or more observable features, such as shape, smell, texture or colour. These may be suggested by the children or by the teacher. The children can then be asked if the fruit can be regrouped according to different features. Children can feel the fruit with their eyes closed or with a blindfold on and consider the texture of skin and smell. They can use their own words to describe the fruit and try to guess which one it is. Other guessing games can also be played. For example, one child may choose a fruit to describe and others can guess which is the chosen fruit.

The fruit can then be cut up and the insides can be observed, again using all senses. The children can now taste a small piece of the fruit and describe what the inside or flesh of the fruit tastes like. Encourage the children to identify whether the fruit tastes different from their expectations or whether the colour or texture is different from the expected. The fruit can then be grouped according to the inside. For example, is the flesh a different colour, smell, taste? How are the pips different? How many pips are there? What does the skin look like? What is the juice like? They can also use their previous knowledge of the fruit, such as whether you can eat the skin, what the pips are like and whether the fruit is grown in this country.

If you are using more unusual fruit you can encourage the children to consider which part of the fruit is edible and which is not. For example, how do you know which part of a passion fruit to eat? What do you do with a pomegranate? Why do you peel a satsuma but not a kumquat?

Recording of the work can take a variety of forms, from simple drawings of fruit to close observational drawings and from drawings of the grouping to tables or Venn diagrams of groups and criteria chosen for sorting.

FUNNY FRUIT

Differentiation

By task: younger children should focus only on the observable features of the fruit, whereas older children may like to consider how the fruit has grown (bananas in bunches, apples on a tree, grapes on a vine; where does a pineapple grow?). Younger children can be asked to record by putting the fruit in groups physically or drawing set maps of the fruit features. Which fruits are tangy, which fruits are yellow, which fruits are soft? Older children may like to record using histograms, detailed drawings or a classification/ identification tree.

Background information

Children will classify and group according to non-scientific principles in the early stages of their educational career. For example, a child may group the fruit into 'those I like and those I don't' or 'those I recognize and those I don't', or 'this is one fruit and all the others are other fruit'. Do not be discouraged, as these are perfectly natural stages. Your encouragement to look at other features will soon allow the child to develop beyond this stage.

The difference between fruit and vegetables is not always apparent and we often use the terms in a culinary sense rather than a biological sense. For example, tomatoes are often thought of as vegetables because they are savoury, but they are fruit. Fruit develops from the flowering body of the plant and contain the seeds necessary to disperse the fruit over a wide area. Flesh that is around the seed is normally designed to attract animals, which aid seed dispersal by eating the fruit and seeds and excreting the seeds at a later time and in another location. However, not all fruits are edible to humans: for example, yew berries and potato apples are not. Berries are fruit, just smaller, with less flesh, and are often found growing on vines or bushes. Nuts are essentially the kernel of the seeds of the flowering plants. There is an almond-like kernel in the hard stone inside a peach. Nuts often have a fleshy outer part, or fruit, which we don't often see, as this is stripped by the time they are on sale in the shops. However, walnuts and sweet chestnuts both have this fleshy outer layer and grow in this country.

Things to notice

Skin. The rind of the fruit serves to protect the soft inner flesh. It can also act as an advertisement for when the fruit is ripe and animals should come to feed. The ripe fruit is normally a different colour from the unripe fruit, so that the unripe fruit is camouflaged against early consumption. The plant also makes the fruit sweetest when it is ripe, so animals are more tempted by the fruit when it is ripe and the seeds are ready to be dispersed. Thick rinds are often a way of discouraging insects from invading and eating the fruit before it is ripe. The outside of the fruit can often tell you how it grew on the plant. For example, apples often have a visible stalk and flower sepals. Pineapples have a visible stalk and grapes are sold in bunches.

Flesh. The flesh of fruits is very variable. Apples and pears have dense, grainy flesh, whereas lemons and oranges have segmented flesh which is made up of small cells. The texture and taste of the flesh is designed to be attractive to one or more species of animal, to aid dispersal.

Taste. The taste of fruits can be very diverse. The classification of these can be very interesting. Citrus fruit have an acidic flavour. Mango has a distinctive peppery flavour and gooseberries have a tart flavour. Blackberries and raspberries are sweet.

Pips. These are the seeds of the plant, and are normally concealed inside the fruit. This is so that fruit will be eaten by animals and the seeds dispersed through their dung. The pips are small, so that they will pass through the stomach tract easily and not be crunched up. As they are small they are numerous, so the plant puts little energy into each seed, as some will inevitably be destroyed. Seeds that are inside the fruit but are large, such as those of mangoes and peaches, have a hard outer shell to prevent them being eaten. In these cases the fruit is designed to attract the animal, which will carry off the fruit and disperse the seeds by throwing them away. Coconuts have evolved so that the outer part of the seed is not fleshy but acts as a buoyancy aid, so the coconut seed (the coconut we actually eat) floats and is dispersed on water. Other plants have developed ways of dispersing their seeds that do not require fruit. For example, some are dispersed in the air (dandelion, sycamore), some mechanically dispersed when the pod dries out and projects the seed away from the plant (laburnum, peas), some are buried by animals in winter storage sites and forgotten (acorns and beech nuts by squirrels) and some are carried on animals' coats (goosegrass, burrs).

What next?

- Make close observational drawings of a variety of fruit.
- Look for patterns in the environment by observing the types of plant the fruit grows on.
- Observe which fruits are ripe at different times of year.
- Play fruit identification games.
- Make a fruit identification key.
- Use a tree database on the computer to compare fruit.
- Observe and sort a collection of fruit and vegetables. Look at what part of the plant the fruit or vegetable comes from.

Other activities that will develop understanding of the different properties of materials

I-spy ice balloons (page 8)
Mixing things (page 18)
Sorting plants (page 36)

Baking changes (page 50)
Dressing teddy (page 54)
Sticky glues (page 64)

Books/stories

Carle, E. (1970) *The Hungry Caterpillar*. Harmondsworth: Penguin.

FUNNY FRUIT

Poems

Never trust a melon, it's a lemon in disguise,
Never trust a potato, with its many eyes,
Never trust a radish that repeats all it hears,
Never trust an onion it will all end in tears.

Is that your apple? In Ahlberg, A. (1983) *Please Mrs Butler*. London: Puffin.

STICKY GLUES

What before?

Kitchen play.

Sticky glues

Look at the different substances with the children and get them to describe the texture of them. Get them to predict which will be most sticky and why. Allow the children to stick two bits of paper together with the substances and test their strength. This could be by hanging weights off the bottom strip of paper, pulling the paper strips apart by hand or a way devised by the children under teacher supervision. Encourage the children to predict, make a fair test and record their findings.

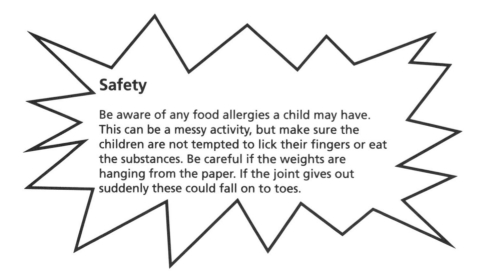

Safety

Be aware of any food allergies a child may have. This can be a messy activity, but make sure the children are not tempted to lick their fingers or eat the substances. Be careful if the weights are hanging from the paper. If the joint gives out suddenly these could fall on to toes.

Resources

Kitchen sauces (for example, ketchup, jam, salad cream, honey, brown sauce, golden syrup, Marmite).
Yoghurt pots.
Lolly sticks or spatulas.
Plain paper.
Squared paper.
Weights.
Sticking tape.
Pens.

Language

Descriptions using own words: sticky, slidey, slimey.
Measuring words, such as weigh, gram, millilitre.

How it fits

With topics

Topics on food and materials.

With National Curriculum

- Sc1, Developing observational skills.
- Sc1, Developing prediction skills.
- Sc1, Developing the skills of recording and communicating.
- Sc3, Developing understanding of *the properties of materials*.
- Eng1, Developing language skills.
- Ma, Developing measuring skills.

With the Early Years Curriculum

Knowledge and understanding of the world.
Language and literacy.
Mathematics.

STICKY GLUES

Setting the scene

Many children will have investigated the sticky qualities of these substances at home and in nurseries, playgroups or schools. However, this activity differs from these experiences because of the focus on the materials and their properties. This is a small group activity, which needs the careful supervision of an adult helper. It is important that you share the learning objectives with the adult helper and discuss prior to the activity questions that would promote learning about materials. The activity can be child-led, where the children are encouraged to think about different ways of testing and the basis on which they judge a substance's stickiness.

Developing children's learning

Language

Encourage the children to describe the different substances using their own words to describe texture. Other non-sticky materials can be used to promote language development if appropriate.

Scientific skills

Encourage the children to observe the different substances and from this initial observation begin to predict which ones will make the best glue. The activity can be good to develop the skill of hypothesizing by asking the children to explain why they think certain substances make good glues.

Scientific conceptual understanding

The main focus of this activity is the understanding of properties of different household substances. In particular, the focus is on the adhesive properties of the substances. This is an interesting activity because it encourages the children to look at the substances and use them in a different way from normal. It also shows that materials may have different properties that are not always recognized.

Mathematics

The children can test the adhesive strength of different substances by seeing how much weight the joint will take. This can be done in a qualitative way, with the children pulling the strips or using a Newton metre, or by hanging weights on the end of the strips.

STICKY GLUES

Attitudes

This activity is good for developing enthusiasm and curiosity. It can also aid perseverance if the children are encouraged to develop their own conclusions and testing mechanisms for the different glues.

Supporting children's learning

The different substances can be put out on the table in their original packaging or a small amount can be placed in a tub or saucer. It is not necessary to tell the children what the substances are. The children should be encouraged in their exploration by asking questions to encourage observation: for example, which substances are slippy, which are sticky? Questions can also be asked to encourage prediction, such as 'Which substance do you think will hold the two bits of paper together best?' Teachers can be good role models by exploring with the children and making some predictions of their own. This will encourage the children to make their own predictions. Children can also be encouraged to communicate why they think a particular substance will make a good 'glue'. Do they think sticky substances make the best 'glue', or thin runny substances, and what is their reasoning? Throughout the activity the children should be encouraged to focus on the different properties of the substances. They can:

- Observe the different substances and describe them using their own words or words introduced to them.
- Look for similarities and differences between the substances.
- Predict which ones would make the best 'glue' on the basis of their observations.
- Explore or investigate the adhesive strength of each substance. This can be done in an exploratory way, but older children may wish to move on to more systematic investigation after an initial exploration. Any investigation can be directed by the teacher or result from the children's own ideas arising from initial exploration and subsequent planning.
- Record the results of any exploration or investigation in a variety of ways. For example, a drawing of the activity with the best 'glue' identified, a poster advertising the best 'glue', a cartoon of the exploration or investigation, or a table of results can all be suitable ways of recording. However, if recording would detract from the experience and the focus of the activity (understanding the properties of materials), then a group or class discussion of findings can be a good way to communicate ideas and consolidate learning.
- Hypothesize as to why the different substances might make a good 'glue'. This can form part of a discussion as described above, and enable the children to interpret from their findings about each substance.

Differentiation

By task: young children can be allowed to explore freely the substances or can be given a predesigned task, such as finding out which glue is best. Recording for younger children is also likely to be through discussion or drawings. Older children will be able to design their own experiment and find their own materials to test. Some children may have difficulty setting up a test.

STICKY GLUES

Encourage them to think of fairness and easy tests even if it is simply to judge by pulling two pieces of stuck paper apart and comparing. Older children can record their findings in a more systematic way through cartoons that sequence the investigation or charts and tables that identify the different properties of each substance.

Background information

All substances are made up of atoms joined together in a particular way to form molecules. Each molecule of a substance is the same and it is the way atoms combine in a numerical pattern which gives each substance its unique characteristics. For example, a molecule of water is made up of two hydrogen atoms and one oxygen atom joined together (H_2O), and a molecule of carbon dioxide is made up of one carbon atom and two oxygen atoms (CO_2). Additionally, substances can exist as solids, liquids or gases. In solids the molecules vibrate to and fro, alternately attracting and repelling, but do not move significantly. In liquids, the molecules vibrate as in a solid, but can also move freely among one another and can therefore take any shape. There are some substances which appear to be solid but are liquid in nature. These are called viscous liquids. For example, glass and pitch appear solid and will smash into small pieces if hit. However, if left for a long time they will also run. This is why glass in very old buildings is thin at the top of panes but thicker at the bottom. A mixture of cornflour and water acts as a viscous liquid, as it can appear hard but will run through your fingers like a liquid. This mixture is also quite a good adhesive. In gases, the molecules are much further apart than in solids and liquids. They move at high velocities, colliding with each other. They are free to expand and fill any vessel and be compressed into smaller containers.

It is sometimes surprising to notice what substances actually make the best glues. Traditional 'sticky' substances such as jam and syrup are not always the best owing to their more liquid nature. Salad cream is often a surprise winner, as is brown sauce. A mixture of flour and water is also extremely good as an adhesive. The success of a particular glue is probably owing to a number of interrelating factors and it is difficult to determine the exact reasons because of the complex make-up of the substances. Some of the possible factors are the amount of starch in a substance, and the amount of liquid in a substance that will evaporate quickly and therefore seal the paper. A substance that does not have a high water content, such as jam or syrup, might not solidify quickly and so will retain its stickiness as well as its slippiness. Salad cream will hold paper together because when the water has evaporated the paper is left stuck together by the starch.

What next?

- Choose a glue for a specific task, such as making a paper bag to hold 25 marbles.
- Test which glue is best if given time to set.
- Try out which substances are the least sticky. This could be done by rolling a toy car down a slope lubricated with the substance under test. Try oil, water, salad cream, orange juice and butter.

STICKY GLUES

- Try some cooking or home kitchen activities.
- Explore a mixture of cornflour and water. Put a drop of food colouring in as well to make it more interesting.
- Explore dough mixtures made with different flours.
- Use the sand tray to explore the properties of wet and dry sand.
- Try finger painting and explore the different consistencies of paint.

Other activities that will develop understanding of the different properties of materials

I-spy ice balloons (page 8)
Mixing things (page 18)
Sorting plants (page 36)
Baking changes (page 50)
Dressing teddy (page 54)
Funny fruit (page 58)

Stories/books

Muir, F. (1983) *What a Mess*. London: Macmillan.
Cole, B. (1985) *The Slimy Book*. London: Jonathan Cape.

FLYING HIGH

What before?

Experience of dropping things.

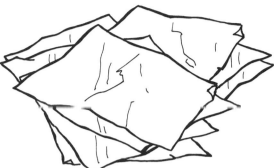

Language

Descriptions using own words: fast, slow, fall, float, drift, fly, glide.

Resources

Scrap paper.
Paper clips.

Flying high

Give each child some paper and encourage them to investigate ways of making the paper fall faster and slower. What things make a difference to the way paper falls? Let the children make paper aeroplanes, either using their own designs or from designs supplied by the teacher, so that the plane will stay in the air for as long as possible.

How it fits

With topics

Topics on travel, flight and air.

With National Curriculum

- Sc1, Developing the skills of predicting and hypothesizing.
- Sc1, Developing the skill of interpreting.
- Sc4, Developing understanding of the *forces involved in dropping things*.
- D&T1, Developing designing skills.
- Eng1, Developing language skills.
- Ma, Developing an understanding of number.
- Ma, Developing an understanding of time and the measurement of time.

With the Early Years Curriculum

Knowledge and understanding of the world.
Language and literacy.

Safety

When launching aeroplanes be careful that no one is in the way.

FLYING HIGH

Setting the scene

This is better as a small group activity, as it might be difficult to oversee the whole class engaged in making and launching paper aeroplanes. One way of organizing the children might be to introduce the activity to the whole class in a systematic way, followed by some individual or small group exploration. In the introduction the children's attention can be focused on how a piece of paper falls normally and how you can change the way it falls. Later the children can experience this for themselves and try out their own ideas to change the way the paper falls.

Developing children's learning

Language

Encourage the children to use their own ideas and words to express the forces involved and the things they notice.

Scientific skills

This activity is a useful vehicle to develop the skills of prediction and hypothesizing. The children can predict, from their own experiences and from the teacher's introduction to falling things, how they can change the way the paper falls and what shape paper aeroplane will stay in the air for the longest time. They can also hypothesize as to why some things are falling at different rates. It is important to remember that their predictions, hypotheses and interpretations do not have to be correct. It is more important that they provide sensible reasons based on their own experiences and the evidence they have.

Conceptual understanding

The main focus for this activity is the forces involved in falling. These are perhaps not as complex as it first appears. Children should notice that objects fall to the ground and that objects with larger surface areas fall more slowly because of air resistance.

Attitudes

This activity is a good one to develop curiosity and respect for evidence. Children will find it difficult to accept that heavy things fall at the same rate as light things even when this is shown to them.

FLYING HIGH

Mathematics

The children can time each aeroplane's fall either by counting or by using a simple stop watch or clock. In this way they will be developing an understanding of time and the measurement of time in standard measures: that is, how many seconds estimated by counting or using a stop watch.

Design and technology

The activity allows the children to design a paper aeroplane and then make and evaluate it. In this way they are beginning to work within the design and technology process and to develop skills in designing and making.

Supporting children's learning

During the teacher introduction it is useful to focus on each stage of the activity carefully and slowly.

- Encourage the children to look closely at one piece of paper falling. How does it fall? Does it fall slowly or quickly?
- Drop two pieces of paper and ask the children to compare the way they fall. Do they fall in the same way? Can you make one piece of paper fall faster than the other?
- Try out the children's ideas and see if they work. You could try: screwing one piece of paper up; dropping one sheet horizontally and one vertically; folding or tearing one sheet of paper.
- It should be then possible to have ideas about what makes a piece of paper stay in the air longer. Ask the children why the different pieces of paper fall at different rates.

Use a sheet of A4 paper

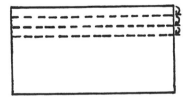

Fold it like this

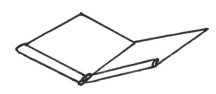

Fold your aeroplane down the middle and try flying it

After the introduction, children can be allowed to try out some of the ideas for themselves and to make paper aeroplane shapes and see how long they stay in the air. You can allow the children to design their own aeroplanes or you could show them a simple folded design (see the Paper Aeroplane Pad published by John Adams Toys). When making a paper aeroplane concentrate on the planes that stay in the air longest rather than the one which flies the furthest. This will reduce the competitive spirit for the best designed plane and focus the children more on the forces involved. Ask the children questions to encourage prediction and hypothesizing. For example, why do they think one particular design will stay in the air the longest? Which aeroplane do they think will fall most slowly? Encourage them to give reasons for any predictions they make. For example, why do they think a particular aeroplane will be best? This will encourage them to give their ideas as to why objects fall at different rates and focus on the forces involved.

Some children will not be able to make an aeroplane that resembles anything much. This does not matter, because it is not necessarily the most sleek planes that will stay up the longest. The aeroplanes made can be tested by releasing all of them at the same time or a small group at a time and seeing which one is the last to land. Alternatively, each aeroplane can be released and its fall timed by counting or with a stop watch. It is important that all the planes get tested so that no child feels her or his effort is worthless.

This activity can also support the development of children's ideas about fair

FLYING HIGH

Take a sheet of A4 paper and fold it in two as shown

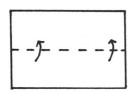

Fold along the dotted line in the direction of the arrow

After each fold turn the paper over and repeat on the other side

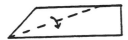

See how your aeroplane flies!

testing. It is clear that the planes have to be dropped from the same height to be fair and have to fall to the ground, not get caught up on a chair or table. By drawing the children's attention to test factors you can get them to begin to consider how to control these variables.

Once the children have found which aeroplanes take the longest time to fall they can begin to interpret from the evidence what the factors keeping a piece of paper in the air are. Encourage the children to share their ideas with others; this will enable them to see that their ideas may not be the same as other children's and may challenge their thinking. Encourage them to focus on possible factors affecting the way things fall, but remember it is not important that their ideas are correct at this stage. If the children hold common misconceptions about falling objects, such as that heavy things fall more quickly than light things, then focusing their attention on exceptions to that rule may help to challenge their ideas. For example, two pieces of paper will fall at the same rate when flat but differently when one is screwed up, although the weight has not changed. You may find that children will say that you have made one piece heavier by screwing it up. You are unlikely to change this misconception by correcting them, but you could ask for other suggestions as to why and challenge their idea with further examples and other objects (see What next?).

Differentiation

By support: with the youngest children more support will need to be given, but later the choices can be made fully independently. Teacher support will also be necessary in the testing of the aeroplanes for all children, although older children will be able to evaluate their aeroplanes more independently.

By task: younger children can explore the paper falling by simple folding or tearing. Older children can be given some designs for aeroplanes to test or they can design their own aeroplanes. Testing for younger children can be very qualitative or by counting seconds. Older children can time the fall of their aeroplanes using a stop watch.

Background information

The focus for this activity is the forces involved in objects falling to the ground, that is gravitational force and air resistance. Gravitational force is the pull on an object due to gravity (which gives the object weight). Gravity itself is a force that is the same for all objects. Weight is affected by gravitational force, which in turn is affected by mass. The larger the mass the greater the gravitational force and the greater the weight. Weight on the Moon will be one-sixth of the weight on Earth because the Earth's mass is six times that of the Moon and mass is proportional to gravitational force. However, when objects fall, the weight does not matter, as gravity accelerates the objects downwards at the same speed.

Gravity exerts a force towards the centre of the Earth on all objects, but when an object falls, air resistance provides a force resisting the descent. The strength of air resistance depends on the size and shape of the moving object. The larger the surface area of the object the more air resistance there will be.

FLYING HIGH

You can observe this when dropping two sheets of paper, identical in weight but with one screwed up. The flat paper has a large surface area and so its air resistance is greater and it will fall more slowly. Weight is not a factor in falling, merely air resistance. This can be seen when dropping two objects which are the same shape and size, but have different weights: for example, a cork and a 100 gram weight. When dropped, both objects will fall at the same rate and hit the ground at the same time. This is because they have the same air resistance acting upon them.

Using these ideas it is clear that often a flat piece of paper will stay in the air longer than any paper aeroplane.

These ideas are often counter-intuitive and appear to conflict with everyday experiences. Children will have observed objects dropping to the ground from an early age and as a result will have developed personal theories about why things fall and what factors affect the rate of falling. Many adults will also hold similar views. In order to modify or change misconceptions such as this and move the children towards a more scientific explanation, it is important to provide experiences that challenge their existing ideas. Children will not necessarily change their ideas just because they are given a new one by their teacher. Sometimes children need a number of very challenging experiences to develop their scientific concepts.

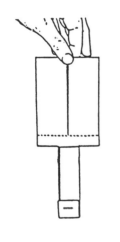

What next?

- Watch a feather fall.
- Make a simple paper helicopter.
- Make parachutes for different objects. Investigate which design is best and which materials are the most suitable.
- Find other objects which are light or heavy for their size and compare the way they fall.

Other activities that will develop understanding of forces

Why do things float or sink? (page 27)   I-spy ice balloons (page 8)
How does it work? (page 82)

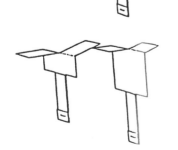

Books/stories

Breathed, B. (1991) *A Wish for Wings that Work*. New York: Simon & Shuster.

Songs

Those Magnificent Men in Their Flying Machines.
Let's Go Fly a Kite.

CAN YOU HEAR ME?

What before?

Listening to sounds.
Sound lotto games.

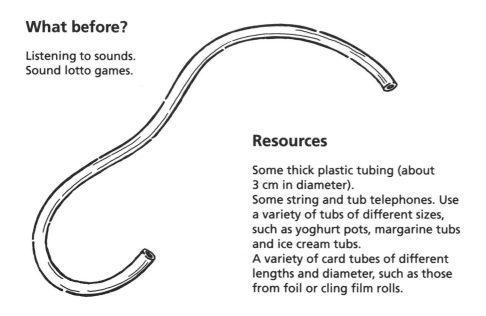

Resources

Some thick plastic tubing (about 3 cm in diameter).
Some string and tub telephones. Use a variety of tubs of different sizes, such as yoghurt pots, margarine tubs and ice cream tubs.
A variety of card tubes of different lengths and diameter, such as those from foil or cling film rolls.

Language

Sound.
Loud, louder.
Soft, softer.
Echo.

Can you hear me?

Allow the children to explore the different 'telephones'. If one child talks quietly down the tubes or into the pots/tubs, she or he can be heard by another child listening at the other end, with the tube, pot or tub to her or his ear. The child can see which tub makes the 'best telephone'.

How it fits

With topics

Topics on sound, noise and communication.

With National Curriculum

- Sc1, Developing observational skills.
- Sc1, Developing exploration skills.
- Sc1, Developing the skills of hypothesizing.
- Sc4, Developing understanding of *sound and how it travels*.
- Eng1, Developing language skills.

With the Early Years Curriculum

Knowledge and understanding of the world.
Language and literacy.

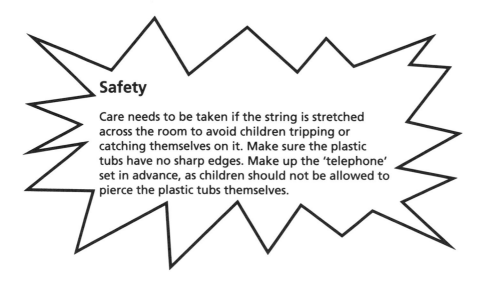

Safety

Care needs to be taken if the string is stretched across the room to avoid children tripping or catching themselves on it. Make sure the plastic tubs have no sharp edges. Make up the 'telephone' set in advance, as children should not be allowed to pierce the plastic tubs themselves.

CAN YOU HEAR ME?

Setting the scene

This activity involves the children experiencing the transmission of sound using a variety of different home-made 'telephones'. The 'telephones' should be already prepared for the children so that they can concentrate on their exploration, notice similarities and differences and hypothesize as to why the telephones work.

Developing children's learning

Language

Allow the children to describe their explorations and hypotheses using their own words. It may be difficult for children to express their ideas initially, so introducing more specific words, such as loud, louder, soft, softer, will help them to develop their ideas. Hypotheses can be expressed as ideas or questions and tested out.

Scientific skills

Observation in this activity will concentrate on sound and materials. Observation of sound can be difficult in a noisy classroom. If children are having difficulty hearing then it would be best to take the group out of the classroom. Simple comparison words can sharpen observations. For example, is the noise louder or softer, clearer or more fuzzy?

Scientific conceptual understanding

The main focus of this activity is understanding that sounds travel away from a source and enters the ear. There is also an opportunity to look at some of the characteristics of sound: that is, that sound is the result of vibrations, it can be loud or soft and it can bounce off objects (echoes) and be contained and amplified.

Attitudes

This activity is a good one to develop enthusiasm and curiosity, as children enjoy exploring sounds.

Supporting children's learning

Allow the children to explore the telephones and to use all their senses in their explorations. This activity is useful to focus on the sense of hearing in observations, and encourages children to listen rather than only to look. Ask the children to describe what they can hear using their own words, and to compare the sounds heard through the telephone to normal speaking sounds. Part of the exploration of the telephones should be focused into hypothesizing. Encourage the children to make a hypothesis as to why one telephone makes a better or louder sound. It might be difficult for children to articulate their hypotheses clearly, and adult help with clarifying their ideas may be necessary. This encouragement can occur with the teacher as a role

CAN YOU HEAR ME?

model. An enthusiastic and sympathetic teacher who does not dismiss hypotheses, however incorrect or odd they may seem, will encourage children to express ideas and begin to look at scientific phenomena in different ways. Ask the children questions to encourage observation and hypotheses, such as 'Does your voice sound different?' and 'Why do you think this "telephone" sounds louder or softer?'

Ask the children further questions to focus on the sound, such as 'What do we have to do to hear the sound?' Sounds travel away from a source and are heard when they enter the ear. Initially children may think that the ear hears the sound rather than the sound entering the ear and being interpreted by the brain. Visual analogies can help to develop a scientific understanding. Try using slinkies or a length of rope to show the way waves travel from the source.

Differentiation

By task: questions can be altered to change the difficulty of the exploration. For example, younger children can be asked to identify the differences between the different telephones. Older children could be asked to find out which telephone makes the loudest sound, or why they think this telephone makes the loudest sound.

By outcome: younger children can explore the telephones and describe their observations using their own words. Older children can be encouraged to be more systematic in their exploration and use more scientific words to describe the sounds.

Background information

A hypothesis is a statement explaining why things happen and normally it can be tested through exploration, investigation or research. 'I think plastic tubs are better telephones than metal tubs, because they make the sound louder' is an example of a hypothesis. Hypotheses do not always need to be correct, but they should be sensible explanations based on the observations and explorations available. When subjected to further exploration and investigation, inadequate hypotheses can be changed or modified in the light of new evidence. Each new piece of evidence builds up conceptual understanding, in this case within the concept of sound.

Sound is a form of energy that occurs as a result of the vibration of molecules. Sound travels away from a sound source in all directions and will pass through solids, liquids and gases, making the molecules of the material vibrate. Each substance it passes through has its own quality, transmitting the sound at different speeds (solids transmit sounds more quickly than liquids and liquids more quickly than gases), and this affects the received sound. When children talk into the tubes the air molecules inside the tube vibrate and these vibrations are partially contained within the tube; this appears to make the sound louder. When children talk into the tub or pot 'telephones' the string vibrates, as do the air molecules inside the tub or pot, which acts like a sound box on a musical instrument, containing the vibrations and making the sound appear louder. Tubs made of different materials will amplify the sounds differently.

CAN YOU HEAR ME?

What next?

- Make different 'telephones' using different materials, for both the tub and the string (e.g. plastic, wood, metal, wool).
- Older children can investigate how the length of the string affects the sound.
- Explore a range of musical instruments and how sounds can be changed.

Other activity that will develop understanding of sounds

Observing around us (page 40)

Other activities that will develop the skill of hypothesizing

Flying high (page 69)   Me and my shadow (page 78)

Song

Beans in Your Ears.

ME AND MY SHADOW

What before?

Looking at your shadows in the playground.

Resources

Some torches.
A projector or overhead projector.
A collection of different objects: for example, wooden or opaque plastic shapes, scissors, toys, transparent plastic drinks bottles, coloured sweet wrappers.
You could also cut out large animal shapes from plastic, greaseproof paper, card, coloured acetates.
A white screen, a sheet of white paper or a white wall.

Language

Shadow.
Light.
Transparent.
Opaque.

Me and my shadow

Allow the children to explore a large collection of objects, using the torches and projector to make shadows. The children can predict which object will make a good shadow and how they can make shadows bigger or smaller. They can then begin to suggest what makes a good shadow.

How it fits

With topics

Topics on light, shadows and toys.

With National Curriculum

- Sc1, Developing observational skills.
- Sc1, Developing prediction and hypothesizing skills.
- Sc1, Developing interpretative skills.
- Sc4, Developing understanding of *how shadows are formed*.
- Eng1, Developing language skills.
- Art, Developing an understanding of shape.

With the Early Years Curriculum

Knowledge and understanding of the world.
Language and literacy.
Creative development.

Safety

Make sure children are aware of the danger of shining lights into eyes and of looking into the projector's light.

ME AND MY SHADOW

Setting the scene

Children will have observed shadows in a variety of contexts, but they will possibly not have looked closely at shadows. A good preliminary activity is to look for shadows in and around the classroom:

- noticing where they are;
- whether you can tell from the shadow what object is making it;
- how dark or light the shadow is;
- how fuzzy or sharp the shadow is.

This will give the children exploration in context, before they progress to a more focused exploration.

Developing children's learning

Language

Encourage the children to describe their observations in their own words, e.g. see-through. Introduce more scientific words, such as shadow, transparent, opaque.

Scientific skills

This activity can help to develop observational skills and also the skill of hypothesizing. Encourage the children to look closely at the objects and resulting shadows and to hypothesize as to why some objects or materials have darker shadows or bigger shadows than other objects or materials. Having explored the different shadows formed, children can begin to interpret from their observations and suggest how shadows are formed.

Scientific conceptual understanding

The main focus of this activity is the understanding that different materials have different transparent, opaque or reflective properties and that they produce different shadows. The children should be helped towards an understanding that shadows are formed when light cannot pass through an object, or when only some light passes through an object.

Attitudes

This activity is useful in helping to develop curiosity.

Art

This activity can be used to look at the shape of objects from shadows. It can be used as an introduction to light and dark in pictures and sculpture.

ME AND MY SHADOW

Supporting children's learning

After giving the children some time to explore the shadows freely, you can help the children to focus their observations on one object at a time, and ask them to predict whether it will make a good shadow. Make your own observations with the children, thus being a good role model. You might wish to draw their attention to the fact that even transparent objects make shadows, and that they can make shadows of different sizes by putting the object closer to the projection surface. Ask the children questions to focus their attention on the shadows and the skills you wish to develop. For example, 'What do you notice about these shadows?' and 'How are these shadows different?' will focus on observations about the different shadows formed by different materials. Asking 'Which object do you think will make a dark/light shadow?' will encourage the children to predict, and 'How can you make the shadow larger/smaller/darker/lighter?' will encourage the children to explore further and try out new ideas. When the children have explored the shadows thoroughly, they can be asked why an object makes the darkest/lightest/smallest/largest shadow, and this will encourage them to interpret as a result of their explorations and consolidate their ideas about shadows and how they are formed.

The children can draw around the shadows and the size of the shadow can be roughly measured, especially if squared paper is used.

Differentiation

By task: young children can be helped to look at different objects and encouraged to describe what the resulting shadow is like. Older children can be asked to find which material makes the best shadow and can then report back on their findings.

By outcome: younger children can discuss their findings in small groups or as a class. Older children can measure shadows and identify through writing and discussion what factors make the best shadows.

Background information

Shadows are formed when light does not pass through an object, leaving a dark patch surrounded by light. This is because light rays travel in a straight line and so cannot reach behind the object. Most objects will make a shadow in a bright light, even if they are transparent. This is because some light will not pass through. Using objects made of a variety of materials enables children to see which materials make the best shadow. The shape of the object can be seen in the shadow. By projecting objects from different angles you can compare shadows. For example, a plastic drinks bottle projected sideways is obviously a bottle, but if projected from the top or bottom the resulting image is quite hard to recognize and has some interesting features. Coloured acetates or plastic will produce some colour on the screen or wall. All acetates allow light to pass through, but it should be possible to see which do so to a lesser degree.

Objects placed close to the light source will make larger, paler shadows with a hazy outline, while objects placed close to the screen and further away from the light source will produce small, dark shadows with firm outlines. This is also due to the characteristic way that light rays travel, in straight lines. When the object is close to the screen, less light can pass behind the object and so the shadow is dark. There is also less scattered light around the edges of the shadow, making them sharp. The shadow is also smaller because only light from the light source at narrow angles is blocked.

What next?

- Make shadows in the playground on sunny days and draw around the shapes. Compare with shadows drawn at a different time of day.
- Try making shadows on different kinds of backgrounds, e.g. black paper, semi-transparent paper or an old white sheet, complete with creases.
- Use mirrors in the exploration, and look at the differences between shadows and reflections.
- Asian cultures have some sophisticated shadow puppet plays, which can be used as a stimulus for making a shadow puppet theatre.
- A simpler alternative is to make shadow animals with cut-outs or just hands, and create a story.

Other activity that will develop understanding of shadows and how they are formed

Recording weather (page 22)

Other activities that will develop the skill of hypothesizing

Flying high (page 69)   Can you hear me? (page 74)

Other activities that will develop interpretation skills

Why do things float or sink? (page 27) Flying high (page 69)
Can you hear me? (page 74)   Bath time for Archimedes (page 86)

Books/stories

Mahy, M. (1982) *The Boy with Two Shadows*. London: J.M. Dent & Sons.

Song

Me and My Shadow.

HOW DOES IT WORK?

What before?

Free play with toys.
Exploration of magnets.
Some simple circuit work.

How does it work?

Put a collection of toys on a table or on the carpet and allow the children some free exploration. Ask them to identify how they work. You can introduce the words magnetism and electricity at this point. Ask the children to sort the objects into two categories according to whether they use electricity or magnetism. During and after the activity discuss with the children how the toys work.

Safety

Be careful with batteries. Do not use rechargeable batteries that may discharge suddenly.

Resources

A collection of toys that use electricity and magnetism. These could include a question and answer box, a magnetic construction set, a magnetic drawing toy, animal shaped magnets, an electrically powered car, an electrical toy which makes a noise or lights up, an electrical spinning top. Children can bring in electrical or magnetic toys from home to add to a collection.

Language

Electricity.
Magnetism, magnetic.

How it fits

With topics

Topics on toys, Victorians (comparisons of toys of today and yesterday) and electricity and magnetism.

With National Curriculum

- Sc1, Developing classification skills.
- Sc1, Developing the skill of raising questions.
- Sc4, Developing understanding of *electricity and magnetism*.
- Eng1, Developing language skills.

With the Early Years Curriculum

Knowledge and understanding of the world.
Language and literacy.

HOW DOES IT WORK?

Setting the scene

The focus of this activity is on looking at magnetism and electricity. Children may benefit from some experience with magnets prior to this activity and some work on using batteries in simple circuits, although this is not essential. Allow the children to play with the toys and experience how they work. They will need very little encouragement at this stage. Later you can ask questions about the toys and introduce the words electricity and magnetism to them.

Developing children's learning

Language

The children may already know the words magnet, magnetism, electric and electricity, but these can be introduced to those who have not met them before and the children can be encouraged to use the words as criteria for sorting the toys.

Scientific skills

Exploration of the toys is a prerequisite of this activity. As has been mentioned previously, exploration is essential for learning, and with this activity the children must be given opportunity to explore the toys fully and to raise questions about them from their explorations, before they can begin to understand the differences between the toys.

Classification can also be developed through this activity, although initially children may wish to classify the toys through other criteria. Focus attention on what makes the toys work, rather than surface features. Some simple magnetic toys, like refrigerator magnets, and simple push button switch lights that do not have distracting features might help to focus the activity.

HOW DOES IT WORK?

Scientific conceptual understanding

The main focus for this activity is an understanding of the uses of electricity and magnetism in toys. Some toys use electricity and magnetism to make them work (move, make a sound, light up), and these toys can be explored to help develop this understanding.

Attitudes

Curiosity is essential for this activity, in that children should be motivated beyond making the toys work to finding out how they work. Curiosity should not be stifled even if it is outside of the focus of the activity, as good scientific learning does not always follow a lesson plan.

Supporting children's learning

Encourage the children in their exploration by pointing out features of the toys, such as 'Look! this one lights up when I do this.' The children should be encouraged to consider how the toys move, what noises they make and what other things they can do, and to raise questions from their exploration that can lead to further exploration. As a good role model, the teacher can raise some questions that will support this. For example, 'Do all the toys have a battery?' or 'Which toys make a noise?' Further questions can encourage the children to sort the toys and develop some classification skills. For example, 'Can you sort these toys into two groups?' 'Can we sort the toys in any other way?'

Some children may not be able to see clearly which toys use electricity and which magnetism. Children can be encouraged to explore the toys by looking for where the batteries might go or trying to find a magnet. Alternatively, magnetic toys will often affect each other so this would be a way of helping a child to find more magnets once she or he has found one. This activity can allow children to work in pairs or groups, and if they are asked to justify their answers this will provide some strategies for supporting those children who are struggling. The development of understanding of the uses of electricity and magnetism can be further supported through discussion of the exploration and the grouping made by the children. Children should be encouraged to explain the criteria for classification and how they think the toys work.

Differentiation

By task: older children can be given more complex toys to explore and can be encouraged (where safe) to look inside the toys to see how they work.

By support: younger children will need more interaction and support than older children. This can be achieved through questioning and adult participation.

HOW DOES IT WORK?

Background information

Electricity and magnetism are closely related concepts, and it is sensible to look at them together in the early stages of development. Both are forms of energy that can be transformed into other forms of energy. For example, electrical energy in an electrically powered car will be transformed into kinetic (movement) energy as the car moves. A question and answer box uses electrical energy, which is transferred into light or sound energy. Magnets use magnetic energy, which is usually transferred into movement or electrical energy. This is used in simple motors, although the toys used here will probably not be examples of this. Some magnetic toys use the attraction and repulsion properties of magnets, and this can be explored with children. Electrical and magnetic energy has a variety of uses in everyday appliances, and this activity focuses on its use in toys, thus setting the activity in a familiar context for the children.

The activity also involves the skill of classification, and further information about this can be found in the activity 'Sorting plants'.

What next?

- Finding other uses of electricity and magnetism in the home or at school.
- Making simple electrical circuits.
- Making electrical and magnetic games/toys, e.g. a steady hand game, magnetic fishing games.

Other activities that will develop classification skills

Dressing teddy (page 54) You and me (page 45)
Funny fruit (page 58) Sticky glues (page 64)
Sorting plants (page 36)

BATH TIME FOR ARCHIMEDES

What before?

Experiences of describing objects.

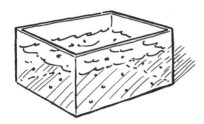

Resources

Archimedes story.
Other science stories.
A plastic tank of water.
A collection of large and small floating and sinking objects: for example, an ice balloon, an air-filled balloon, a water-filled balloon, a brick.
Waterproof marker pens.

Language

Experiment.
Invention.
Overflow.

Bath time for Archimedes

Read the story of Archimedes to the children. Discuss what it might have been like to live at the same time as Archimedes. Encourage children to say what it is like when they think deeply about things. Set out a number of large objects on a table with a tank of water, and help the children to observe and measure displacement. Measurements can be made by marking the level of the water on the side of the tank using the marker pen. Encourage them to make predictions based on their observations. Get them to report back to others on their discoveries, make a story of their exploration or use the story and their exploration in role play.

How it fits

With topics

Topics on scientific discovery and inventions.

With National Curriculum

- ScPoS, Developing an understanding of *science in everyday life*.
- ScPoS, Developing an understanding of *the nature of scientific ideas*.
- Sc1, Developing observational skills.
- Sc1, Developing the skills of interpretation.
- Eng1, Developing speaking and listening skills.
- Hi, Developing an understanding of the lives of famous people.

With the Early Years Curriculum

Knowledge and understanding of the world.
Language and literacy.
Mathematics.

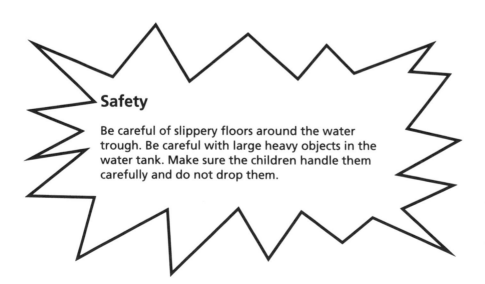

Safety

Be careful of slippery floors around the water trough. Be careful with large heavy objects in the water tank. Make sure the children handle them carefully and do not drop them.

BATH TIME FOR ARCHIMEDES

Setting the scene

This could be a whole class activity that can encourage cognitive, affective and creative development and prevent science becoming a purely practical exercise. Although hands-on activities are imperative for good learning, a story at the beginning and a 'non-scientific' outcome such as a piece of creative writing may increase the children's enjoyment of science and help them to understand the nature of science. When you read the story, encourage children to answer the questions and ask questions of their own. This will help to provide a focus when they are engaged in the activity. Emphasize the need to think carefully about things, so that the focus of the activity remains exploratory rather than one of finding out the 'correct' answers.

The following story can be read to the children.

Bath time for Archimedes

Archimedes lived more than two thousand years ago in Greece. He was a clever man who was famous for his inventions and his experiments. He thought about things very carefully and looked at things very carefully too.

One day Archimedes got into his bath and noticed that the water level had risen. He may have filled the bath too full and it had spilt over the sides.

'Why has that happened?' he thought.

He thought about it for a long time until his bath water was very cold. Eventually, after lots of thinking, Archimedes thought 'I bet that if I was bigger, the water level would rise even higher. If I was smaller, the water level would probably not have risen so high.'

After you have read the story, the children can explore the ideas using the water trough or a tank of water, and record and communicate their ideas through writing, drawing, discussion or role play.

BATH TIME FOR ARCHIMEDES

Developing children's learning

Language

The children can be introduced to scientific words – such as invention, investigate and displacement – during the story, with exploration as appropriate. They should have opportunities to use these words in retelling the story and in role play situations.

Scientific skills

This activity is useful to develop observational skills through exploration in the water trough or tank. In the follow-up discussions the children can use their experiences to make some simple interpretations about what happens to objects when placed in water.

Attitudes

The main focus for this activity is understanding of the nature of science and recognition that science plays a large part in our everyday lives. Bath time is an everyday occurrence that nearly all children will be familiar with (some will take showers), but they may not have had the opportunities to look at the science underpinning such an everyday phenomenon.

History

Through this activity children can be introduced to the life of one famous scientist. Children can also begin to consider the part Archimedes has played in developing the scientific understanding that we have today.

Supporting children's learning

When exploring displacement, it is a good idea to concentrate on objects that sink when placed in water. This will help the children and prevent confusion. Displacement is a complex idea and it is not necessary for children to understand the principles involved. Children should be encouraged to look closely at the water level in the trough or tank and to watch it change as objects are placed in the water. Observe with the children and ask them questions such as 'What do you notice about the water level?' and 'What happens when I put a big object in the water?' This will help them to focus their observations.

The activity is designed to develop an understanding of the history and nature of science. It particularly focuses on ways of looking at everyday phenomena, such as the displacement of objects in water. It is important for children to have access to the stories of science, so that they understand that scientists come from many different backgrounds and had to think very hard to get an answer that fitted their observations. Even then, they were often wrong, but this didn't matter. The stories of science show that science is not only for scientists and results can be presented in a number of ways.

Discussions following the activity can focus on the exploration and how Archimedes reached his conclusions as a result of his experiences. Children could be asked what happens to the water when they get into the bath or what they think would happen to the water level if two people were in the bath. Children can also pretend to be Archimedes in a role play situation and to make new scientific discoveries for themselves.

Differentiation

By support: younger children will need a lot of support during the exploration. This can be achieved through questioning and adult participation. Older children will be able to be more independent in their explorations.

Background information

Archimedes is best known for discovering the law of hydrostatics, often called Archimedes' principle. It is this law that he is supposed to have discovered when he stepped into a bath and it overflowed. What Archimedes discovered was that when an object sinks or is immersed in water it displaces (pushes out of its way) a volume of water equal to the object's volume.

Displacement is, in many ways, another aspect of floating and sinking. It focuses on the water rather than the object itself, and also links with measuring volume. It can help in the development of concepts such as weight, mass, density and volume, as well as looking at forces. This activity is therefore one that can be returned to, as the children develop more sophisticated concepts, looking each time at fresh aspects.

The Archimedes story focuses attention on the value of thinking deeply, observing carefully and then experimenting to test out your ideas. In this way the activity should reflect this sequence by allowing the children to think about what happens in the bath or a washing up bowl, observing carefully what happens when different objects are put into water. Science involves thinking deeply and looking carefully at everyday phenomena in different ways. Sometimes we become so familiar with things around us that we don't think about them or understand them. Archimedes was famous for a number of reasons, but one of them was that he didn't just think about things, he also tried them out. He also made close observations of the results of his experiments. Archimedes often became so involved in his ideas that he forgot about the world around him. During a war between Carthage and Rome a Roman soldier found Archimedes working out a mathematical diagram in some sand. Archimedes was so absorbed in his thinking that all he said was 'Don't disturb my diagram', and this annoyed the soldier, who killed him.

It is useful for children to listen to someone else's experience and to think about their own experiences. It is important for children to feel that they can 'do' science anywhere, and look at a variety of things scientifically. It is also good to encourage them to think hard because often, when presented with an activity, children would rather act than review what they already know and use this to guide their actions.

Science is not a subject that many children associate with stories. However, it is very important for children to understand the history and nature of science so that they understand that science is not only the prerogative of scientists. One criticism of school science is that it lacks relevance. Looking at the part science plays in society through history can help children to see the relevance of science. Using commonplace imagery to illustrate scientific principles helps to emphasize the everyday nature of science and promotes scientific understanding.

What next?

- Look at floating objects and the water displaced by them.
- Use a margarine tub floating in a water trough or tank. Explore displacement by adding marbles.
- Try floating things in another liquid, such as cooking oil.
- Look at some inventions of Archimedes. For example, you could look at levers. Collect some household objects that use the lever mechanism and allow children to explore their use.
- Write a story or draw a picture about Archimedes or a wonderful discovery that you have made.

Other activities that will develop an understanding of the nature of science and the part science plays in everyday life

Darwin has an idea (page 91)   James Barry's secret (page 96)

Books/stories

Allen, P. (1980) *Mr Archimedes' Bath*. London: Hamish Hamilton.
How Things Work CD-ROM.

DARWIN HAS AN IDEA

What before?

Looking at different groups of animals.
Some ideas about where different places are in the world.

Resources

Pictures of animals.
Identification books.
A globe or world map.

Language

Evolution.
Explore.
Names of places.
Names of animals.

How it fits

With topics

Topics on Victorians and animals.

With National Curriculum

- ScPoS, Developing an understanding of *science in everyday life*.
- ScPoS, Developing an understanding of *the nature of scientific ideas*.
- Sc1, Developing observational skills.
- Sc1, Developing the skill of classification.
- Eng1, Developing scientific language.
- Hi, Developing an understanding of the lives of famous people.

With the Early Years Curriculum

Knowledge and understanding of the world.
Language and literacy.

Darwin has an idea

Show children pictures of animals and discuss with them similarities and differences. Encourage them to categorize in different ways: for example, by appearance or by what part of the world they come from. Share Darwin's story with them. Encourage them to discuss animal families and classification. Discuss the differences between animals in relation to where they evolved.

Safety

Be aware that some religions still hold a scriptural view of creation, and will not accept this theory of evolution. Provide this story as an alternative view rather than the only and correct view.

DARWIN HAS AN IDEA

Setting the scene

Look at pictures of animal families with the children before telling them the story, and look for similarities and differences between the animals.

The following story can be read to the children.

Darwin has an idea

Charles Darwin was a rich young man who lived over a hundred years ago. Charles was very interested in science and the world around him. He had the opportunity to go on an exploration ship to sail around the world. The ship was called the *Beagle*. Charles wanted to look at all the animals around the world and take notes about where they lived and what they liked to eat. The ship sailed for weeks and weeks. It stopped in South America and then sailed on until it reached a small group of islands called the Galapagos Islands. Here Charles studied the birds and other fascinating animals. The animals on the island were truly amazing. There were giant tortoises the size of coffee tables, iguana lizards that swam in the sea, sea birds that couldn't fly and lots of other birds. It was the birds that Charles was really interested in. He saw how each little island had slightly different birds on it, and then he thought a bit more and a bit more and some more until his head ached. He thought about the books he had read and the ideas that other people had had and then he thought of an idea that was very exciting.

He thought that the birds were all alike enough to be members of a family, but like a family each one was a bit different. The reason they were different, thought Darwin, was that each one had a slightly different home. Each one lived in a special way and wouldn't fit in as well on another island. It was as if a mother bird and a father bird had lots of babies that had flown away to live on other islands, and each one had grown up differently, depending on what the island was like. On his other travels he had noticed how birds in different countries sometimes looked similar. The emu in Australia looked a lot like the rhea in South America and the African ostrich. These birds were very similar, but different too.

Charles thought of the idea that these birds that looked alike perhaps all had the same great-great-great-great-great-great-great-great-great-great-great until you run out of greats grandparents, and had just lived so far apart for so long that they had grown to look different. Each type of bird had grown to suit where it lived, and though they were related to each other, they wouldn't want to live in the other birds' country.

Charles wrote a book about his ideas, which we now call evolution. This was very upsetting to some people, who didn't like the idea that humans could be in the same family as monkeys. Who wants their great, great, great, great, great grandfather to be a monkey? They were very angry and it caused a lot of argument, and some people still argue about these ideas today. However, lots of people agreed with Charles, and more evidence was found that supported his idea. Today most people agree with Charles's ideas, although some investigation is still going on.

A caricature of Charles Darwin drawn by 'Ape' which appeared in the magazine *Vanity Fair* after an historic debate on evolution organized by the British Association in 1860.

DARWIN HAS AN IDEA

Developing children's learning

Language

Encourage the children to listen to the story. They can try to retell the story to others. Further discussion about animal families can help them to develop new vocabulary and to clarify their ideas.

Scientific skills

This activity is useful in developing observational skills, through observing similarities and differences between animals. It is also useful to develop classification skills.

Conceptual understanding

The activity can help in the development of understanding about the adaptation of living things to their environment.

Attitudes

The main focus for this activity is understanding of the nature of science and recognition that science plays a large part in our everyday lives. Charles Darwin was a man who developed his ideas as a result of observations made throughout his life. He had to persevere to get his ideas accepted by others, and this emphasizes two important scientific attitudes: perseverance and respect for the ideas of others.

History

Through this activity children can be introduced to the life of a famous scientist. Children can also begin to consider the part Darwin has played in developing the scientific understanding that we have today.

Supporting children's learning

Encourage the children in their observations of animal families to look for similarities and differences. You can use a wide selection of animals but you might use pictures of animals that have obvious similarities and differences. These could include:

• a horse, a donkey and a zebra;
• a rhea, an ostrich and an emu;
• a dog, a wolf, a fox and a Tasmanian tiger.

Ask the children to describe the similarities and differences between the animals. Ask them to group the animals according to their similarities and differences.

Tell the children the story and use the animal pictures to support you. You can encourage and motivate the children by pointing out that they too had the same idea as Darwin, and so are obviously thinking very scientifically. Point out to the children that not everyone agreed with Darwin's ideas and that even today some people have different views. This will help them to realize that scientific ideas are continually developing. They will also begin to see the tentative nature of scientific ideas.

Differentiation

By support: the amount of support given to the children during the story telling and discussion will vary according to age and ability.

By outcome: younger children will probably group the animals according to one or two observable features. Older children will be able to classify the animal pictures using a variety of different criteria.

Background information

Charles Darwin lived from 1809 to 1882. He was an English scientist who was meticulous in his observations of natural phenomena. When he was 22 years of age, Darwin joined the English survey ship *HMS Beagle* as an unpaid naturalist. The *Beagle* was engaged in a voyage of scientific discovery around the world, and Darwin was able to observe geological formations on different continents and look at fossils of long extinct animals, as well as living animals. Until this time most geologists held the view that the Earth had experienced a number of creations, but that each one had been destroyed by some catastrophe, such as earthquake or flood. This theory explained why some animals were now extinct. Darwin's observations led him to question some of these ideas and to consider the ideas of natural selection and common ancestry. As a result, Darwin developed the modern theory of evolution and supported previously held ideas that the Earth is not static but continually evolving. Animals have to compete for survival and those with characteristics that support survival will live and pass on those characteristics to their offspring. The principle of natural selection, which Darwin proposed with Alfred Russel Wallace, aroused bitter controversy because it disagreed with the literal interpretation of the Book of Genesis in the Bible. There were some very public disputes, with the most famous being at a meeting of the British Association in Oxford in 1860. Samuel Wilberforce, Bishop of Oxford, asked T. H. Huxley (a supporter of Darwin's ideas) if he was descended from a monkey on his grandmother's or grandfather's side. Huxley responded by stating that there was nothing to be ashamed of in having an ape as an ancestor.

It is important to note that there are still many people who do not fully accept Darwin's theories. It is also important to note that the theory is still evolving and that Darwin's original theory does not completely explain the evolution of all animals, plants and insects. Genetic research is making headway into this area.

This story helps to identify the tentative nature of science. There are often different interpretations of scientific phenomena, and we should respect evidence and the ideas that others hold. Science cannot be seen as simply a body of facts to be learned that explain the world, but as a complex interrelationship of ideas that are constantly changing in small ways.

What next?

- Make a cartoon of Darwin's voyage and discoveries.
- Record the sorting exercise using Venn diagrams.
- Find out about other Victorian scientists.

Other activities that will develop an understanding of the nature of science and the part science plays in everyday life

Bath time for Archimedes (page 86)   James Barry's secret (page 96)

Other activities that will develop the skill of classification

Sorting plants (page 36)   Sticky glues (page 64)
You and me (page 45)   How does it work? (page 82)
Dressing teddy (page 54)

Books/stories

Kipling, R. (1982) *Just So Stories for Little Children. How the Leopard Got His Spots*. London: Macmillan.
Lear, E. (1973) *The Quangle Wangle's Hat*. Harmondsworth: Puffin.

JAMES BARRY'S SECRET

What before?

Other stories of scientists.

Resources

The story of Dr James Barry.

Language

Medicine.
Doctor.
Hygiene.
Hospitals.

James Barry's secret

Tell the children the story of Dr James Barry. Talk to them about the main points of the story and ask them questions about the story. Ask them to retell the story in words and pictures. Set up the play area as a hospital or doctor's surgery.

How it fits

With topics

Topics on medicine and Victorians

With National Curriculum

- ScPoS, Developing an understanding of *science in everyday life*.
- ScPoS, Developing an understanding of *the nature of scientific ideas*.
- Sc1, Developing the skills of recording and communicating.
- Sc2, Developing understanding of the need for hygiene for healthy living.
- Hi, Developing an understanding of the lives of famous people.

With the Early Years Curriculum

Knowledge and understanding of the world.

Safety

This activity can illustrate the need for hygiene for good health. It can also lead to discussion about equal opportunities, but care needs to be exercised to avoid presenting children with opinions about these issues.

JAMES BARRY'S SECRET

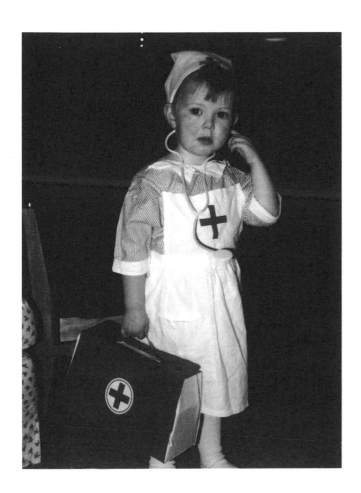 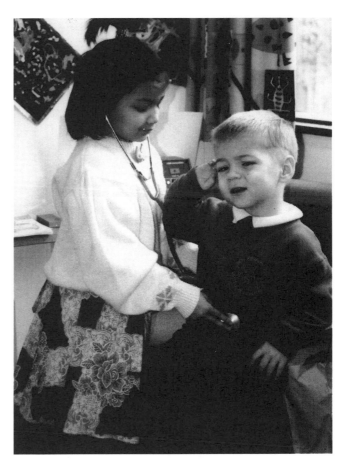

Setting the scene

This activity focuses on the history and nature of science, but will also lead to opportunities to consider the importance of hygiene to healthy living. The story can be told to the children during story time.

James Barry's secret

James Barry was a doctor. He worked in a hospital. The hospital was not very clean and there were lots of germs. The germs made people ill. Doctor Barry liked to be clean. He washed his hands when he operated on people. He made the nurses keep the hospital clean and many people got better. Doctor Barry had a secret. Everyone thought that he was a man but he was not. Doctor Barry pretended to be a man because women could not be doctors. When James was born her parents sent her to live with friends and be brought up as a boy. She wore boys' clothes and had her hair cut like a boy. She studied very hard and learnt lots of things. She studied to be a doctor and everyone believed that she was a boy. She could not tell anyone that she was really a girl because then she would not be allowed to work in the hospital as a doctor. When she died the other doctors were very surprised. They did not think that girls were clever enough to be doctors. Today hospitals are much safer and cleaner places. James Barry helped to make hospitals safe and clean and changed people's ideas about women as doctors.

When the story has been read you can discuss the main issues with the children, encouraging them to express their opinions. The children can then retell the story in words, pictures or a cartoon format.

Set up the play area in the classroom so the children can re-enact the story or pretend to be doctors.

Developing children's learning

Language

Encourage the children to listen to the story. They can try to retell the story to others.

Scientific skills

This activity is useful in developing recording and communicating skills. Recording of the story can be oral, written, pictorial or through role play. The children can communicate their ideas about the nature of science (for example, why women can or cannot be scientists) in class discussions.

Conceptual understanding

The story can help to develop understanding that hygiene is an important part of healthy living.

Attitudes

The main focus for this activity is an understanding of the nature of science and recognition that science plays a large part in our everyday lives. Changes in our understanding of health and hygiene have had a large impact on our lives, and this can be discussed as a result of this story. Ideas of equality and respect for others are equally important.

History

Through this activity children can be introduced to the life of a famous scientist. Children can also begin to consider how medical science and the views of society have changed since James Barry's death.

Supporting children's learning

Once the story has been told to the children, encourage them to help in the retelling by asking them questions such as 'What happened next?' Questions are also useful to clarify the main issues of the story or the children's understanding. For example, 'Why did Doctor Barry pretend to be a man?' or 'Why should you keep your hands clean?' Children will have their own experiences of visits to the doctor or to the hospital. Sharing these experiences can help children to see the medical advances that have occurred over the past century. They will have experienced the importance of cleaning cuts and keeping their hands clean to avoid the spread of disease. They will also have met women doctors. Ask the children to imagine what it would have been like to have been ill 100 years ago, or what they would have felt like to be James Barry. The children can record and communicate the story in a variety of formats:

- Tell the story to someone else. This could be in a whole class situation where retelling the story could be shared by all the children in turn.
- Guided or independent writing of the story as part of the class's literacy hour.
- Make a cartoon of the story.
- Draw an annotated picture of a hospital.
- Use the play area as a hospital.

Throughout this activity, it is important that children are not indoctrinated with one particular viewpoint, but are allowed to reach their own conclusions about James Barry's unusual life.

Differentiation

By support: the amount of support given to the children during the story telling and discussion will vary according to age and ability.

By outcome: older children will be able to produce more advanced writing when retelling the story. Younger children can draw an annotated picture to help in the retelling of the story.

Background information

James Barry was born as a girl. Her parents wanted her to be well educated and sent her away to a foster home, where she was brought up and educated as a boy. The more educated she became, the more difficult it became to disclose her real identity. She wanted to become a doctor, and continued to pretend to be male. She eventually became a doctor and worked in a hospital as a surgeon. She is famous for introducing strict hygiene and cleanliness into the hospital, making sure that surgical implements and surgeons themselves were clean before operations. As a result, she was able to carry out the first successful birth by Caesarean section, with both mother and child surviving. Before this, mothers usually died because of unhygienic practices and subsequent infections. During her life James Barry kept a diary, which told of her secret life and the difficulties of pretending to be male. When she died her secret was discovered, and the medical fraternity suppressed the knowledge because they felt that it was impossible for a woman to have succeeded in medicine as James Barry had done. Her diaries have recently been acknowledged, and her place in medical history is now recognized.

This story can raise some very complex issues, which are appropriate for discussion at any age. It can inform us about the influence of beliefs and values on scientific understanding and help us to see that medical science has advanced considerably. Through such stories, children can develop a better understanding of how science has progressed through history and the relevance of scientific discovery on their lives. Issues such as equal opportunities for scientific knowledge and professions can be discussed, and children can consider how attitudes towards equal opportunities have changed over time. It is through such discussions that children can develop awareness of the differing beliefs and ideas that others hold, and are able to formulate their own ideas based on experiences and simple scientific knowledge. This is an important aspect of being a citizen of the future, making informed decisions based on evidence and after consideration, and recognizing the part society plays in influencing ideas and beliefs.

The story can also lead on to discussion about the relationship between health and hygiene. Washing hands and disinfecting surfaces and implements are important to prevent the spread of disease. Knowledge of the role of hygiene in the prevention of disease has developed as a result of scientists like James Barry. Sterilization of medical implements to avoid the spread of disease is well known in our society, but medical knowledge was not as clear on the subject before the twentieth century. The effects of poor hygiene can be seen in news reports around the world after major catastrophes, such as earthquakes, floods and war.

What next?

- Look at a collection of plants and animals traditionally used for medicinal purposes. You could use: liquorice sticks (available from health food stores), which help digestion; a foxglove, as digitalis extracts help to regulate the heart; some maggots (available from an angling shop), which were (and are) used to clean infected wounds.
- Look at dental hygiene.

Other activities that will develop an understanding of the nature of science and the part science plays in everyday life

Bath time for Archimedes (page 86)   Darwin has an idea (page 91)

Other activities that would develop the skill of recording and communicating

Recording weather (page 22)   You and me (page 45)
Body mapping (page 31)   Funny fruit (page 58)
Sorting plants (page 36)   Sticky glues (page 64)

Poem

In came the doctor,
In came the nurse,
In came the lady with the alligator purse.
Naughty said the doctor,
Naughty said the nurse,
Naughty said the lady with the alligator purse.
Out went the doctor,
Out went the nurse,
Out went the lady with the alligator purse.